Special Considerations for Students With High-Functioning Autism Spectrum Disorder: A Guide for School Administrators

Diane Adreon, Ed.D.

Brenda Smith Myles, Ph.D.

T0126294

©2017 Diane Adreon and Brenda Smith Myles
www.fhautism.com
info@fhautism.com
817.277.0727

Table of Contents

Purpose of This Guide

■ ■ ■

Autism spectrum disorder (ASD) is a fact of everyday life in today's schools. Yet, despite increased public awareness and education surrounding ASD, many school administrators do not have sufficient tools to address the unique challenges posed by students with ASD and the dynamics of most classrooms.

This guide provides useful and practical suggestions and strategies geared for school administrators. Specifically, the tools are designed to:

- Increase achievement, engagement, positive behavior, and social skills for high-functioning students on the autism spectrum (HF-ASD);

- Help reduce educator stress and frustration; and

- Increase positive interactions between families and school personnel so that the school day is more successful for all parties.

Recognizing the competing demands on administrators' time, this brief and targeted book highlights information specific to students with HF-ASD without repeating common information that applies to students with other disabilities.

Introduction

■ ■ ■

Schools serve a diverse group of students, including students with disabilities. In recent years, the prevalence of autism spectrum disorder (ASD) has been the subject of considerable media coverage. Now reported in 1 out of 68 individuals in the United States, the term "ASD" is used to reflect the range of abilities and symptoms demonstrated by this group, 69% of whom have IQ scores above the cut-off for intellectual disabilities (Centers for Disease Control and Prevention, 2014).

Previously, the diagnostic manual used by medical doctors and psychologists included several specific subtypes of the general diagnosis of autism, so students in your school may have paperwork stating that they have Autism or Autistic Disorder, Pervasive Developmental Disorder-Not Otherwise Specified (PDD-NOS), Pervasive Developmental Disorder (PDD), and Asperger's Disorder or Asperger Syndrome (AS). The new label does *not* mean, however, that the behaviors of these children has changed.

To some extent, this disability is "hidden" in that the strengths of this group of students often mask areas in which they have true deficits. For example, on the surface, the communication skills of students with HF-ASD may appear adequate. In fact, many students with HF-ASD have impressive vocabularies and may even sound advanced for their chronological age. However, in reality, they may simply be repeating what they have memorized and have little understanding of what they have said. Similarly, they may be able to repeat a passage from a textbook without understanding what it means. In addition, students with HF-ASD often have difficulty understanding idioms and the use of sarcasm (Whyte, Nelson, & Khan, 2013). As a result of these factors, you may assume that these students have a higher level of skills than they actually do.

For these and other reasons, students with HF-ASD often pose significant challenges for school personnel because, in many cases, common education practices do not significantly increase their achievement or reduce the challenging behaviors these students often display.

This book provides specific information school administrators can utilize to build their school's capacity to work effectively with students with HF-ASD and in the process reduce teacher stress and burnout.

CHAPTER 1

"High Functioning" Does Not Mean That Students Don't Have Significant Challenges or Areas of Strengths

■ ■ ■

This chapter provides an overview of the characteristics of students with high-functioning autism spectrum disorder (HF-ASD) and how these characteristics are manifested in the school setting. In addition, the numerous strengths of students with HF-ASD are addressed, including ways in which these strengths can be utilized to improve their achievement in school.

Autism spectrum disorder (ASD) is a developmental disability characterized by

- Poor social and communication skills

- Sensitivity to various sensory experiences

- Rigid adherence to particular routines or rituals and/or obsessive interests that are abnormal in intensity or focus (American Psychiatric Association [APA], 2013).

In addition, individuals with ASD commonly experience behavior (cf. McGuire et al., 2016) and motor (cf. Sumner, Leonard, & Hill, 2016) challenges.

ASD is not an "emotional disturbance," nor is it caused by poor parenting. Current research suggests that ASD is a neurodevelopmental disorder with a genetic and environmental component (cf. Kim & Leventhal, 2015). The characteristics of ASD, and specifically those of individuals with HF-ASD, need not limit their potential if appropriate instruction and supports are provided. The following is a brief description of the characteristics of students with HF-ASD that impact school performance.

Social and Communication Skills

Individuals with HF-ASD have poor social skills and often do not understand social expectations in various situations. For example, the student may not know that there are certain things that you might say to a peer but that it would be inappropriate to say to the principal.

> *Judy Endow, an adult with HF-ASD, reports that she didn't know that the teacher was the most important person in the room until she was in high school. Image how much confusion she experienced and how much trouble she probably got into, because she did not know that she needed to listen to and follow teacher directions.*

Individuals with HF-ASD also have difficulty in understanding how others perceive situations.

> *Ben, a student with HF-ASD, was reading a book about the Civil War after he finished eating his lunch in the cafeteria. When Alex, one of his classmates, started talking to him, Ben said, "Alex, can't you see I'm busy reading?" Ben did not*

understand that his comment might hurt Alex's feelings. Fur-thermore, he did not realize that such behavior will decrease the likelihood that Alex will initiate conversations with him in the future. Not surprisingly, this type of reaction contrib-utes to problems related to making and keeping friends.

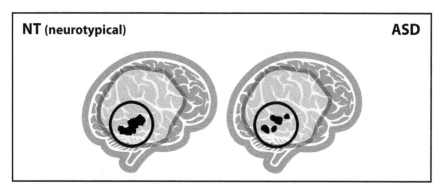

The above brain scans show social perception circuit activity in boys with ASD and those without. The image on the right clearly illustrates the lack of continuity in the social circuity of individuals with ASD (Richey et al., 2015).

Frequently, these students interact more successfully with adults or children who are younger than they are. Sometimes, their social interactions are perceived by as rude or defiant although this is not their intent.

> *Sam, a boy with HF-ASD, said to Mrs. Smith, his fourth-grade teacher, "Why do you continue to eat so much? You're very overweight." Sam didn't understand why that would be an inappropriate comment to make to his teacher. After all, Mrs. Smith is overweight, and he couldn't understand why she wasn't doing something about it.*

Almost all students with HF-ASD fail to understand that nonverbal cues such as facial expressions, gestures, proximity, and eye contact convey meaning and attitudes. Students with HF-ASD miss out on many social opportunities because they do not "get" the important parts of communication. That is, they often cannot read facial expressions, gestures, and so forth.

> *Jay is drawing at his desk while his teacher, Mr. Hawkins, is talking to the class. Mr. Hawkins walks over to Jay and stands with his arms crossed and a stern look on his face. Mr. Hawkins expects Jay to know that he is upset. Moreover, he expects Jay to know that he should not be drawing at this time. Jay, however, does not understand that Mr. Hawkins is communicating without words.*

> *Johnny, a student with HF-ASD, notices that Katie, a girl in several of his classes, frequently glances over at him and smiles. Johnny does not realize that these behaviors are signs that Katie likes him.*

On the surface, the communication skills of students with HF-ASD may appear adequate. In fact, many students with HF-ASD have impressive vocabularies and may even sound advanced for their chronological age. However, their expressive skills often mask their comprehension problems. Literal thinking is a hallmark of students with HF-ASD. Therefore, they often have difficulty understanding idioms and the use of sarcasm.

> *Mr. Thomas thinks that Tim is a "smart aleck" because of the way he responds in class. One day, when Mr. Thomas asked Tim if he had the time, Tim merely said yes. He did not realize that Mr. Thomas was actually asking what time it was.*

Sensory Issues

Up to 95% of students with ASD have sensory challenges (Baker, Lane, Angley, & Young, 2008; Myles, Mahler, & Robbins, 2014). For example, studies, including neurological studies, have reported challenges in the sensory systems related to sound (cf. Green et al., 2013); touch (cf. Green et al., 2015); movement and sense of body in space; balance (cf. Marko et al., 2015); taste and smell (cf. Ashwin et al., 2014; Bennetto, Kuschner, & Hyman, 2007); sense of internal organs, including skin (cf. Fiene & Brownlow, 2015); and sight, with the visual system touted as a strength (cf. Soulières et al., 2009).

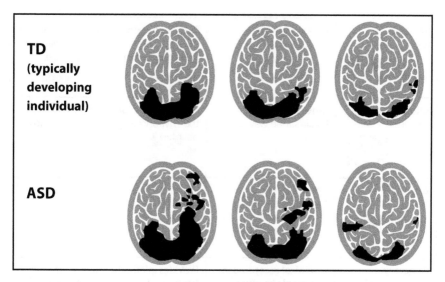

The previous figure shows how certain brain regions react more to noise in individuals with ASD than in neurotypicals (Green et al., 2013). The following is a brief overview of the locations and functions of the sensory systems, including interoception – the internal state and condition of the body – which has been incorporated in recent years.

System	Location	Function
Tactile (touch)	**Skin** – density of cell distribution varies throughout the body. Areas of greatest density include mouth, hands, and genitals.	Provides information about the environment and object qualities (touch, pressure, texture, hard, soft, sharp, dull, heat, cold, pain).
Vestibular (balance)	**Inner ear** – stimulated by head movements and input from other senses, especially visual.	Provides information about where our body is in space, and whether or not we or our surroundings are moving. Tells about speed and direction of movement.
Proprioception (body awareness)	**Muscles and joints** – activated by muscle contractions and movement.	Provides information about where a certain body part is and how it is moving.
Visual (sight)	**Retina of the eye** – stimulated by light.	Provides information about objects and persons. Helps us define boundaries as we move through time and space.
Auditory (hearing)	**Inner ear** – stimulated by air/sound waves.	Provides information about sounds in the environment (loud, soft, high, low, near, far).
Gustatory (taste)	**Chemical receptors in the tongue** – closely entwined with the olfactory (smell) system.	Provides information about different types of taste (sweet, sour, bitter, salty, spicy).
Olfactory (smell)	**Chemical receptors in the nasal structure** – closely associated with the gustatory system.	Provides information about different types of smell (musty, acrid, putrid, flowery, pungent).
Interoception (inside body)	**Inside of your body** – helps the body "feel" the internal state or conditions of the body.	Provides information such as pain, body temperature, itch, sexual arousal, hunger and thirst. It also helps bring in information regarding heart and breathing rates and when we need to use the bathroom.

From Myles, B. S., Mahler, K., & Robbins, L. A. (2014). *Sensory issues and high-functioning autism: Practical solutions for making sense of the world* (2nd ed.). p. 10. Reprinted with permission.

Special Interests

A core characteristic of students with HF-ASD is intense interests and a love for sharing facts and figures related to these special interests. Interests are diverse, including (a) transportation, (b) machines and technology, (c) dinosaurs, (d) history and culture, (e) videogames, (f) sports, (g) people, (h) science, (i) games, (j) animals, (k) art, and (l) motion pictures. The special interests of boys on the spectrum often are different from those of their neurotypical counterparts. However, the interests of girls tend to mirror those of their same-age, same-gender peers with an emphasis on (a) animals, (b) books, (c) art, (d) dress-up, (e) nature, (f) music, and (g) movies (DeLoache, Simcock, & Macari, 2007; Jordan & Caldwell-Harris, 2012; Winter-Messiers, 2014).

Further, challenges in social skills, including reading others' nonverbal behaviors, often lead to one-sided monologues about special interests because the student cannot monitor whether the listener is interested or not.

> *A group of middle-school girls were overheard talking between classes. As Lori, a girl with HF-ASD, rounded the corner, Nicole said to her friends, "Don't even look at her or slow down because she will start talking about Egypt and mummies. She doesn't know that we could care less."*

Behavior

Approximately 50% of students with HF-ASD demonstrate behavior challenges (cf. Mazurek, Kanne, & Wodka, 2013) that include melting down, withdrawing from others, or lashing out toward others. These behaviors are neurologically based and, therefore, not willful. They are usually due to low frustration tolerance, poor coping skills, weak problem-solving, and difficulty reading the social cues of others (Myles et al., 2005). In fact, individuals with HF-ASD are often reacting to a world around them that they see as unpredictable, unforgiving, and cruel.

Considering the pressures listed below, it is no wonder many students experience meltdowns or other seemingly excessive behavioral reactions:

- Failure to understand rules and routines
- Desire for friendships coupled with few skills to make this happen
- Disruptions from pursuing an all-encompassing special interest
- Stress related to coping with the everyday challenges of change
- Inability to protect oneself from teasing and bullying.

The circled areas in the figure below represent a composite of fMRI scans showing the areas of the brain that are significantly less active in people with ASD during emotion regulation and, therefore, affect behavior (Richey et al., 2015).

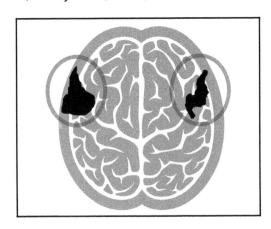

When something changes in the environment (i.e., the teacher is absent, a field trip is canceled, the lunch menu changes, or the classroom furniture is rearranged), even changes that most students would find favorable (there is an assembly during math class or a class party instead of language arts), students with HF-ASD may become upset, possibly triggering a meltdown. Such a reaction makes sense when we realize that research shows that individuals with HF-ASD experience "minor changes" similarly to the way most people experience major changes – such as the loss of a job (Gomot & Wicker, 2012). Imagine how you would feel if you processed minor changes in this way! It would be exhausting and overwhelming.

> *Miguel's class was planning to go to the science museum. He was especially excited about seeing to the dinosaur exhibit. When he was told that the field trip was canceled due to a schedule change, he started screaming to his teacher, "You lied! You said we were going to the science museum." Then he threw himself on the floor saying over and over again, "We were supposed to go to see the dinosaurs … we were supposed to go to see the dinosaurs."*

High levels of stress, anxiety, and depression are prevalent among those with HF-ASD. In fact, approximately 80% experience one or more of these conditions (Salazar et al., 2015), but the way they demonstrate them can be deceiving. For example, a student may indicate stress by laughing or exhibit an air of superiority when confused. Therefore, it is important that others around them – parents, siblings, teachers, and peers – know what signs to look for. Unlike many typically developing peers, students with HF-ASD may not reveal their emotions through voice tone, body posture, and so forth. Because their cues are so subtle, their agitation often escalates to a point of crisis before others become aware of their discomfort.

> *Al, a middle-school student with HF-ASD who is enrolled in advanced content courses, is academically capable of completing most of his work. However, his teachers expressed concerns about what they termed Al's "unpredictable tantrums." They were ready and prepared to prompt him to home base (see page 44), when necessary, but most of the time they were unable to detect the signs leading up to an approaching tantrum. One of Al's teachers, Mr. Moore, noted that it appeared as if Al's meltdowns came from nowhere. As a result, the teachers were surprised to hear from Al's mother that he had a definite stress signal – when he ran his hand through his hair, it meant that he had "had enough." Recognizing this small cue helped Al's teachers to prompt him to home base, thereby preventing the occurrence of meltdowns. A program was also put in place to help Al recognize his own behavioral signal so that he could monitor his stress level himself.*

Motor Skills

Many students with HF-ASD have problems with fine-motor skills, such as tying shoes, manipulating buttons and snaps on clothing, cutting with scissors, and handwriting. In many instances, their handwriting is illegible. Surprisingly, some have exceedingly neat handwriting, but that comes at a great cost. Their hands fatigue easily, and it takes them a long time to produce written work. Research suggests that the handwriting of these students does not improve significantly despite interventions and the best of efforts and that, therefore, it is more effective to teach them keyboarding early on (cf. Kushki, Chau, & Anagnostou, 2011; Myles et al., 2003).

Many students with ASD have poor gross-motor skills as well (Fournier, Hass, Naik, Lodha, & Cauraugh, 2010). They often seem to walk in the path of others and tend to drop things or carry them in an awkward manner. Not surprisingly, in school, physical education (PE) class is particularly problematic. Changing into gym clothes often takes students with HF-ASD an inordinately long time. In addition, a general lack of close supervision in the locker room places these students in a vulnerable situation where social difficulties may surface.

Further, the awkwardness that results from difficulty with motor activities that involve multi-tasking, such as group sports, coupled with their poor social skills, often makes students with HF-ASD the target of bullies. Too often, these students are "picked last" for teams, and PE may be a class that contributes to their low self-esteem (Memari et al., 2015).

Academics

As a result of the myriad characteristics of autism, students with HF-ASD experience academic challenges as described in the following table.

Characteristic	Example of Impact on Learning
Limited attention span	May miss presentation of content information because thoughts are elsewhere. Because of a lack of awareness that information has been missed, will not seek it out.
Difficulty knowing what to focus on and what to ignore	Focuses on how many horses died during Custer's Last Stand and does not understand the events that led to the event and its outcome.
Reading comprehension problems masked by average to above-average word-calling skills	When asked a question, can use rote memory to "recite a fact" but has challenges in (a) drawing inferences, (b) sequencing events, (c) understanding cause and effect, (d) interpreting character motivation, and (e) using prediction and other complex reasoning skills.
Motivation to focus on a special interest instead of teacher-directed tasks	When reading about Valley Forge and the American Revolutionary War, focuses on frostbite because it is related to a special interest in weather. Does not understand that the reading goal is to focus on George Washington's leadership skills during this event.
Lack of understanding regarding teacher expectations and other unwritten rules	May talk out in class when teacher "expects" the students to be quiet. May not know when the teacher does not want to answer student questions. Does not understand why she cannot be in charge of the cooperative group she is in. When the teacher says, "You cannot ask questions during the examination," student does not understand that she cannot ask content-related questions, but can ask to sharpen pencil.
Poor organizational skills	May miss a math problem because he cannot organize information on the page, such as lining up numbers to complete a math operation. Has problems organizing thoughts and creating an outline for a paper.
Difficulty processing auditory information with reliance on visual information to learn	Learns little from teacher oral lectures, particularly when the lecture also contains (a) idioms and metaphors, (b) sarcasm, (c) complex humor, and (d) information that incorporates complex structure and content.
Knowledge of rote (or memorized) tasks instead of conceptual tasks that require an in-depth understanding and manipulation of knowledge	Appears to have a lot of information about a topic, but when analyzed, this knowledge is often a recitation of facts and memorized sentences. Often cannot synthesize and apply information. For example, can recite the dates of Shay's Rebellion, its location, and who was involved as well as one or two memorized sentences from the text on this subject. However, cannot understand why this clash threatened to disunite states unless this is directly stated in the text. Also cannot compare and contrast Shay's Rebellion and the Boston Tea Party.
Motor and processing issues may result in a slower work rate and less production	Focuses on forming letters rather than content. Finishes work with fewer words – long after the other students have completed their work.
Problems completing homework	Parents may indicate that (a) child needs downtime at home, (b) they do not understand homework, (c) too much time is required for homework, and (d) student completes homework but does not turn it in.

Hudson, J., & Myles, B.S. (2007). *Starting points: How to understand and support children and youth with Asperger syndrome* (pp. 47-48). Adapted and reprinted with permission.

Most typically developing students enjoy the unstructured times of the school day. In contrast, for those with HF-ASD, these situations are often stressful and increase their anxiety levels. Common problem times include:

- Riding the bus
- Before class starts
- Transition times (when moving from one activity to another)
- Passing periods (when students are moving from one class to another)
- Recess
- Lunch
- Physical education
- Specials (music, art)
- Special events (field trips, assemblies, class parties)

The Cumulative Effect

The characteristics and examples described above are presented as if they occur in isolation. But they do not! As the environment becomes complex, involving many people, noise, and other stimuli, the skills of students with HF-ASD seem to deteriorate.

Mrs. Rice, the language arts teacher, is confused by Tara's inconsistency in social and language skills demonstrated during class activities. Before school, when the two of them are alone, Tara and Mrs. Rice had a fairly complex conversation about Greek myths. Mrs. Rice felt that Tara demonstrated good language comprehension and social skills.

However, at the end of class, Tara did not get her homework planner signed by Mrs. Rice. She did walk up near the teacher's desk waiting for the opportunity to ask Mrs. Rice to sign the planner, but she was unable to ask her question because other students were asking questions, too. When the bell rang signaling the end of class, Tara took that as her cue to leave and left without getting her planner signed – all because she didn't know how to enter into the conversation.

The Strengths of Students With HF-ASD

Students with HF-ASD are often described in terms of their deficits and challenges, but they have many strengths and abilities. Unfortunately, these strengths are often overlooked when, in fact, they can be used as the basis for building new skills. Areas of strength include:

- Attention to detail
- Intensive knowledge about items of special interest
- Strong visual skills
- Highly developed verbal skills
- Effective direct communication skills
- Average to above-average intelligence
- Ability to conform to clearly stated rules
- Good rote memory
- Honesty and trustworthiness
- Punctuality

- Loyalty
- Detailed factual knowledge in narrow areas
- Exceptional concentration, especially for areas of interest
- Reliability
- Technical ability
- Creativity
- Not launching unprovoked attacks
- Genuineness
- Caring and helpfulness, when recognizing the need
- Original perspectives on issues
- Predictability
- Ability to entertain self
- Not taking advantage of others' weaknesses
- Consistency
- Lack of interest in "office politics"
- Preference for active learning (cf. Autism Topics, n.d.).

There are numerous ways these strengths can be utilized within the school setting and serve as the basis for learning new skills. For example, incorporating special interests into class- or homework can greatly enhance the motivation of the student with HF-ASD to actively participate, focus, and complete a task. For example, having a student with HF-ASD prepare and deliver a presentation on a topic of interest can provide an opportunity for her to learn to speak in front of the class. The student whose visual strength is manifested by his extraordinary drawing ability might be asked to draw the illustrations for a short story, whereas another student's ability to create intricate Lego models might be incorporated into an assignment about various types of architecture.

Summary

HF-ASD is a complex neurologically based disorder. While students with this disorder have many challenges that differentiate them from their nondisabled peers, it is important to recognize that they also have many strengths. Understanding the characteristics of HF-ASD makes it possible to provide appropriately for these students to help them reach their limitless potential.

CHAPTER 2

Important Considerations for Educating Students With HF-ASD

■ ■ ■

This chapter targets information specific to the education of students with HF-ASD. The first section identifies the elements that predict future employment and independent living for those with HF-ASD. These predictors are useful in developing and implementing educational programs. In addition, issues related to assessment, placement, bullying, and discipline are discussed because they are often misunderstood and can significantly impact students on the spectrum.

Predictors for Life Success

Most likely you entered the field of education to help students, including those with HF-ASD, become successful adults. Unlike other areas of education, there is no set curriculum or list of courses to follow to attain this goal. Fortunately, in recent years the National Technical Assistance Center on Transition (NTACT; n.d.) has identified a number of research-based guidelines that schools can adopt to support students in these areas. These are reviewed below (http://transitionta.org).

- **Support of parental involvement and expectations.** Parents should be encouraged to take an active role in their children's school life. The outcomes of such involvement include higher grades and test scores as well as increased student motivation (cf. Rowe et al., 2015).

- **Authentic community-based work experiences.** Students with disabilities, including those with HF-ASD, who participate in paid employment and work experiences in high school are more likely to be engaged in post-school employment and education, and to live independently. Authentic community-based work experiences include job sampling, job shadowing, internships, apprenticeships, and paid employment (Wehman et al., 2014).

- **Social and emotional instruction.** A direct link exists between social and emotional skills and a broad range of health, social, and economic measures (cf. Jones, Greenberg, & Crowley, 2015; Shanker, 2014). Because these are typically skills that are not automatically well developed in learners with HF-ASD, ongoing direct instruction must be provided.

- **Self-determination/independent living instruction and skills building.** Self-determination – the ability to make choices, solve problems, set goals, evaluate options, take initiative to reach one's goals, and accept consequences of one's actions – is a challenge for most students with HF-ASD. When coupled with direct instruction on the skills required for independent living, self-determination training supports adult success (cf. Bethune & Test, 2014).

- **Academic/vocational/occupational/educational prepara-tion.** Students need to develop a wide range of so-called soft skills, such as problem-solving, communicating with supervi-sors and colleagues, being courteous, responding positively to constructive criticism, following directions, and being punctu-al. In addition, they need to learn skills such as résumé writ-ing, dressing for success, specific occupational skills, practical math, and using public transportation. Instruction on some of these skills can begin in early elementary school (cf. Council for Exceptional Children's Division of Career Development and Transition [CEC/DCDT] Publications Committee, 2014).

- **Collaborative network of student support.** Networks should include family, educational professionals, service providers, and friends. For students with HF-ASD, effective student networks in-clude Circles of Friends, Lunch Bunch, Special Interest Clubs, and so forth (cf. CEC/DCDT Publications Committee, 2014).

- **Individualized career development.** Strategies, supports, and services should be aligned with the student's learning style and provide access to careers that reflect the youth's preferences, interests, and skills. While this may include the student's special interest, it should also incorporate introduction to careers with which the student has little or no familiarity (cf. Ohio Employ-ment First, n.d.).

- **Inclusive practices and programs.** To the extent possible, stu-dents with HF-ASD should be included in general education classes. The more hours students with special needs spend actively engaged in general education classes, the more likely they are to be living independently and have employment once they leave school (cf. Chiang, Cheung, Hickson, Xiang, & Tsai, 2012).

These elements should be considered throughout the learner's school experience as they can significantly affect quality of life, including future relationships, employment, and independent living. In addition, the remaining topics in this chapter also need to be considered as they impact the student's school experience and have been found to be critical to school and later life success, in particular for students with HF-ASD (cf. Grossman & Aspy, 2011).

Assessment

As shown in Chapter 1, individuals with HF-ASD demonstrate myriad characteristics specific to the autism spectrum as well as co-occurring conditions. Unless school assessment teams are comprehensively trained to understand the many manifestations of HF-ASD, a student with this disorder may be misidentified as having a speech-language disorder, emotional disturbance, or attention deficit-hyperactivity disorder (ADHD). In fact, the first label a child with ASD is likely to receive is ADHD (cf. Miodovnik, Harstad, Sideridis, & Huntington, 2015). Such misidentification can result in (a) the development and implementation of an inappropriate school program that does not meet the learner's needs, (b) a frustrated learner whose needs are not met and whose challenges continue to escalate, and (c) upset family members who feel that they are not being heard by the school. It takes a well-trained team to see beyond individual characteristics to fully understand the various manifestations of the autism spectrum.

Placement

The majority of students with HF-ASD attend general education classes. Due to their excellent long-term rote memory skills and their tendency to excel in specific areas of academics, many function well in several aspects of school. In addition, because students with HF-ASD are usually of average to above-average intelligence, most benefit from attending classes with content that is on or above their grade level. For example, if the student has a relative strength in math or reading, her participation in class not only strengthens her math skills but may also help to build her self-esteem (Barnhill, 2004).

However, these skills are not sufficient. Since social-communication challenges are one of the core deficits of students with ASD, these students need to learn to interact with typically developing peers. This is consistent with *The Individuals With Disabilities Education Act* (IDEA; 2004), which stipulates that to the maximum extent appropriate, children with disabilities should be educated with children without disabilities. However, as for all students with special needs, placement decisions should be made by a team, including family members, based on individual student strengths and needs.

Some students on the spectrum exhibit behavioral challenges and, therefore, are in need of special support. Unfortunately, the majority of programs designed to serve students with behavior disorders or emotional issues are not appropriate for students with ASD. In part, this is because many students attending those programs are socially savvy and often victimize students with HF-ASD. In contrast, students with HF-ASD are socially naïve, cannot interpret social situations, and easily become prey for others (Volkmar, Klin, Schultz, Rubin, & Bronen, 2000).

Students with HF-ASD should be placed in an environment that provides supports and instruction that matches student need with multiple opportunities for positive practices and strong role models.

Bullying

"My grandson, Noah, a 10-year-old with HF-ASD, is currently in a psychiatric hospital because his only option for the bullying he suffered at school seemed to be suicide." (Appleford, 2014)

The National Education Association (NEA; n.d.) defines bullying as:

… systematically and chronically inflicting physical hurt and/or psychological distress on another. Bullying can be physical, verbal, or social. Bullying is not just child's play, but a frightening experience many students face every day. It can be as direct as teasing, hitting, threatening, destruction of property, or forcing someone to do something against their will, or as indirect as in rumors, exclusion, or manipulation. Bullying involves a real or perceived power imbalance between the one who bullies and their target.

In addition to the above examples, harassment is also a form of bullying. It is important to recognize that for a behavior to be considered harassment, it does not have to include the *intent* to harm, be directed at a specific target, or involve repeated incidents (U.S. Department of Education Office of Civil Rights [USDOE OCR], 2014).

Bullying and harassment are common forms of violence among children, and although there has been an increased focus on bullying in recent years, administrators often underestimate the extent of bullying in their schools. The following provides an overview of the prevalence of bullying in schools

- 22% of middle- and high-school students are bullied (Institute of Education Sciences [IES] National Center on Statistics, 2016)

- Of these students, 33% are bullied at least once a month, and 6% are bullied every day (IES National Center for Education Statistics, 2016)

- 63% of students with ASD have been bullied (Interactive Autism Network, 2014)

- 50% of students with ASD are at risk of being bullied, regardless of age or gender (Maïano, Normand, Salvas, Moullec, & Aimé, 2016)

Where does bullying occur in schools? The short answer is: Everywhere! The table below lists the locations where bullying is most likely to happen, along with the corresponding percentages.

School Locations Where Bullying Occurs

Location	% Who Are Bullied
Hallway or stairway	46
Classroom	34
Outside on school grounds	23
Cafeteria	19
Bathroom or locker room	9
School bus	8

From Institute of Education Sciences National Center on Statistics. (2016). *Indicators of school crime and safety: 2015.* Washington, DC: U.S. Department of Education, U.S. Department of Justice Office of Justice Programs. Reprinted with permission.

Students with ASD are particularly vulnerable to bullying because of their poor social and interpersonal skills and their low self-esteem. Therefore, it is important to ensure that strategies are in place to prevent bullying, including (a) making sure certain students are not seated together at the same lunch table, (b) allowing the target student to wait for the bus near a designated staff member, or (c) having hallway monitors in place during passing times. In some instances, it may be necessary to rework a student's schedule so that the perpetrator(s) of bullying is(are) not in the same class as the victim.

> *"We never would have known that another child had his hands around our son's neck and was choking him if another parent hadn't called us. The school's response only occurred because we found out and insisted that something be done. Our child does not like school and is afraid while he is at school."* (Parent of a 6-year-old student with HF-ASD; cited in Massachusetts Advocates for Children, 2009)

When a student with a disability is bullied, the individualized education program (IEP) or 504 team should convene to ascertain whether ...

- The bullying has resulted in a denial of a free and appropriate public education (FAPE) because the student's academic, emotional, or behavioral performance has deteriorated;
- The student's educational needs have changed;
- The student needs additional or different services.

These steps will help ensure that the student is receiving FAPE (USDOE OCR, 2014).

In addition, the following strategies have been shown to help reduce bullying in schools: (a) adopt a school-wide bullying program; (b) conduct school-wide bullying prevention activities; (c) increase adult supervision in all common areas, such as hallways, stairwells, cafeteria, bathroom, and locker room; and (d) establish a protocol for investigating reported instances of bullying (cf. Humphrey & Hebron, 2015).

Heinrichs (2005) developed the Modified Inventory of Wrongful Activities, an interview, to help administrators obtain useful information from a student with HF-ASD regarding possible instances of bullying. (This instrument may be found in Appendix A.)

Several other resources have great value for administrators. These include:

- *Bully Prevention*, a positive behavior intervention and support (PBIS), designed to help students and other bystanders who observe bullying to respond (http://www.pbis.org/common/ pbisresources/publications/bullyingprevention_ES.pdf)

- *Bully Police USA*, an overview of each state's policies against bullying (www.bullypolice.org)

A Final Note

A lack of understanding on the part of staff regarding bullying can create situations in which adults unintentionally become perpetrators. Because adults, and especially administrators, set the tone in the school for how *all* children are perceived and treated, it is important to provide instruction and resources to help staff understand and avoid what may be "subtle aspects of bullying," such as use of sarcasm.

Bully at the Blackboard (http://www.tolerance.org/bully-at-black-board) is an excellent resource for adults. Finally, *Recognize, Respond, Report: Preventing and Addressing Bullying of Students With Special Needs* (Ernsperger, 2016) includes an array of strategies and resources for school and classroom as well as individual interventions.

Discipline Issues

When an educator asks, "Is it the autism or is it the behavior, 99.99% of the time it is the autism." (Ruth Aspy & Barry Grossman, The Ziggurat Group; personal communication, October 2016)

"Typical" discipline procedures, such as in-school suspension, are rarely effective in changing the behavior of students with ASD because they do not teach new skills. The most effective strategies are usually grounded in the reasons why the offending behavior is occurring in the first place.

It is easy to misunderstand the behavior of students with HF-ASD. Despite having an average to above-average IQ, their social maturity and understanding of general social behaviors and rules tend to be one third to two thirds younger than their chronological age.

Note

If students with HF-ASD break a rule or engage in inappropriate behavior, it is best to assume that they did not understand the rule – even if they can state it. For students with ASD, there is a disconnect between being able to state what to do and actually doing it. And discipline will NOT teach them what to do. The best way to address this issue is through (a) prevention and (b) instruction.

For additional information on how to address behavior issues, we recommend that you refer your staff to the following resource, *High-Functioning Autism and Difficult Moments: Practical Solutions for Meltdowns* (Myles & Aspy, 2016).

Many of the challenging behaviors exhibited by students with HF-ASD can be anticipated when the school team has a solid understanding of the characteristics of students with HF-ASD, as well as the environments within the school that are challenging for them. The IEP team needs to be proactive and anticipate the issues that are likely to arise. Schools that have embraced PBIS are in the best position to address the needs of all students who exhibit challenging behavior.

If school officials do not understand the reason for a given behavior, a functional behavior assessment (FBA) may be a logical next step. Aspy and Grossman (2011) developed a framework for conducting an FBA to assess and design a behavior intervention plan (BIP) based on the characteristics of students with ASD, including those with HF-ASD (Aspy, Grossman, Myles, & Henry, 2016). Appendix B provides an overview of this process.

Suspension and expulsion. Schools may suspend students with disabilities for up to 10 consecutive days and follow normal due process procedures, assuming the district would apply similar consequences for students without disabilities. In the event that a student is suspended for less than 10 consecutive days but for a total of more than 10 school days during the school year, the issue becomes whether this pattern constitutes a change of placement. If the student is removed for 11 or more consecutive school days, the removal is considered a change of placement, and a manifestation determination meeting must be held within 10 days (Massachusetts Department of Education, 2007; Osbourne & Russo, 2009).

During a Manifestation Determination Review (MDR) hearing, all relevant information is reviewed, including the relationship between the student's disability and the target behavior (IDEA). *The Underlying Characteristics Checklist – High Functioning* (UCC-HF; Aspy & Grossman, 2007) is an extremely helpful instrument in determining whether a given behavior infraction is, indeed, related to the student's ASD (see the following sample).

UCC-HF
UNDERLYING CHARACTERISTICS CHECKLIST-HIGH FUNCTIONING
Ruth Aspy, Ph.D., and Barry G. Grossman, Ph.D.

NAME: _____ DATE: _____ COMPLETED BY: _____

FOLLOW-UP DATE: _____ COMPLETED BY: _____

INSTRUCTIONS FOR COMPLETING INITIAL ASSESSMENT:
The UCC may be completed by an individual; however, the perspective of others who know and/or work with the person of focus is beneficial. Working as a team is optimal. Additionally, the team may include the individual who is the focus of the UCC as developmentally appropriate.

Each item describes behaviors or characteristics that may be exhibited by individuals with autism spectrum disorders. Please place a check beside ALL items that currently apply to the individual. Use the *Notes* column to describe the behavior and characteristics in more detail, provide specific examples, or indicate frequency, settings, etc.

Projected **Follow-up** date: _____

Area	Item	✔	Notes	Follow-Up
SOCIAL	1. Has difficulty recognizing the feelings and thoughts of others (mindblindness)	✔	• *Does not recognize when classmates tease or "set her up"* • *After being corrected at home, she repetitively asks her parents if they are still angry* • *In role plays, she can accurately identify the feelings of others 4 out of 10 times*	
	2. Uses poor eye contact			
	3. Has difficulty maintaining personal space, physically intrudes on others	✔	• *Sniffs peers' hair*	

INSTRUCTIONS FOR FOLLOW-UP ASSESSMENT:
Review checked and unchecked items. Use the *Notes* column to add further descriptors or to indicate changes. If item no longer applies, strike through the check and explain changes in the Follow-up column, as illustrated below.

Area	Item	✔	Notes	Follow-Up
SOCIAL	1. Has difficulty recognizing the feelings and thoughts of others (mindblindness)	✔	• *Does not recognize when classmates tease or "set her up"* • *After being corrected at home, she repetitively asks her parents if they are still angry* • *In role plays, she can accurately identify the feelings of others 4 out of 10 times*	• *Accurately reported that she was being teased last week* • *In role plays, she can now accurately identify others' feelings 6 out of 10 times*
	2. Uses poor eye contact			
	3. Has difficulty maintaining personal space, physically intrudes on others	✗	• *Sniffs peers' hair*	• *No longer sniffs others. Follows rules for respecting personal space of others*

From Aspy, R., & Grossman, B. G. (2007). *The underlying characteristics checklist – High-functioning (UCC-HF)*. Reprinted with permission.

In addition, the Student Perspective Analysis (see Appendix C) is helpful for understanding how the student perceives the school day, thereby getting a better insight into his behavior. Specifically, items are designed to elicit the student's likes and dislikes related to peers, teachers, and social and academic demands as well as to provide information on each of his classes.

If it is determined as a result of the MDR that a given misbehavior was a manifestation of the student's disability, the student cannot be expelled, and the district needs to determine if the behavior was the result of the district's failure to implement the student's IEP. If so, immediate steps should be taken to remedy the situation.

Restraint and seclusion. Seclusion and restraint are highly dangerous techniques, having led to death, injury, and trauma in children. At least 20 children have died in restraint, and others have been injured and died in seclusion (Butler, 2015). It is important to note that prone (lying face down) restraints are particularly dangerous for students with HF-ASD because of their low muscle tone. For these students, restraint could result in serious injury or death.

To prevent deaths and injuries, the U.S. Department of Education (2012) has identified the following important considerations regarding the administration of restraint and seclusion:

1. Restraint or seclusion should be avoided to the greatest extent possible without endangering the safety of students and staff.

2. Physical restraint or seclusion should **not** be used except in situations where the student's behavior poses imminent danger of serious physical harm to self or others.

3. Restraint and seclusion should be **discontinued as soon as imminent danger of serious physical harm to self or others has dissipated.**

4. There is **no** evidence that restraint and seclusion are effective in reducing problem behaviors.

5. Restraint and seclusion should **not** be used as discipline or punishment.

6. Restraint and seclusion should **not** be used to address inappropriate behavior such as disrespect, noncompliance or insubordination.

7. Restraints that restrict a student's breathing should **not** be used because they can cause serious injury or death.

8. Every instance in which restraint or seclusion is used should be visually monitored to ensure the appropriateness of its use and the safety of the student, other students, teachers, and other personnel.

9. Parents should be notified as soon as possible following each instance in which restraint or seclusion is used with their child.

Most inappropriate behaviors of students with HF-ASD can only be addressed in an effective manner through instruction and practice. In addition, it is essential that instruction occurs when the student is calm and, therefore, is ready to learn.

Summary

Fostering a school environment that comprehensively addresses the key predictors for life success will positively impact students' post-school outcomes. In addition, proactively addressing bullying; rethinking ineffective discipline procedures such as suspension, restraint, and seclusion; and focusing efforts on fully implementing PBIS will improve the behavior of students with HF-ASD as well as other students in your school.

CHAPTER 3

Strategies for Working With Families of Students With HF-ASD

"I would like school if there were no other students."
– 16-year-old Margot with HF-ASD

■ ■ ■

Students with HF-ASD require higher "maintenance" through-out their lives than many professionals realize. In general, getting through the school day is often so taxing for these students that they barely have any reserve energy left once they get home after school. As a result, it is a major struggle for many parents just to get through morning and evening routines with their child with HF-ASD.

Families of students with HF-ASD are often confused and frustrat-ed over the mismatch between their children's intelligence and strengths and the tremendous difficulty they have in performing tasks in school and the community that "appear simple." In many instances, these parents are highly invested in their children's success and are constantly in contact with school personnel to discuss social challenges, as well as obtain clarification about aca-demic assignments.

As if all this wasn't challenging enough! Research suggests that there is a strong genetic component to ASD; therefore, it is not unusual for some family members to exhibit some of the traits of their student with ASD. In fact, it has been suggested that characteristics of the disorder are present in first-degree relatives (Ingersoll & Weiner, 2013). Similarly, Kanner and Asperger noted that many parents of children with ASD had traits reminiscent of autism (cited in Silberman, 2015). This manifestation of traits is referred to as the "broad autism phenotype" (Ingersoll & Weiner, 2013).

The upshot is that, on occasion, school personnel may find themselves dialoguing with a parent whose interactive style is inflexible and perhaps even offensive due to inherent ASD traits. All of these factors can contribute to strained relationship between parents and teachers, administrators, and school staff as they try to teach, meet the needs of all students, and communicate effectively with students' families.

> *"Before they [parents] care how much you know, they gotta know how much you care!"* (Lavoie, 2008)

Strategies That Foster Effective Family-School Relationships

Here are some strategies for successfully working with families.

- **Train your staff in implementing teach-back.** Teach-back is an evidence-based intervention that can lay the groundwork for better communication, mutual understanding, and shared decision making. Although originally developed for communication between healthcare providers and patients, these tools are equally applicable in educational settings. Teach-back strategies are simple and effective with an emphasis on the use of simple language and having the listener rephrase what the speaker has said. Free training materials are available to help you and your staff master teach-back strategies and evaluate the implementation of teach-back in your school (Agency for Healthcare Research and Quality, 2016).

- **Strengthen your partnership with parents.** According to IDEA, parents are equal partners in making educational decisions for their children. However, often home-school communication is one-sided and school-directed. The vast majority of poor family-school relationships, as well as due process cases, are the result of poor communication (Lavoie, 2008). Solicit family members' input about their child's needs and supports. Ask them what strategies have worked at home and which ones have not. Find out what school interventions could impact home life. Listen to family members and incorporate their input into the IEP and the student's school day.

- **Encourage your staff to listen empathically to parents and fully hear their concerns without becoming defensive.** Start with the assumption that the parent has a valid viewpoint. Listening is key to establishing trust and building a good relationship. Everyone has a need to be validated. Parents' struggles are real, and their perceptions are their reality.

- **Motivate and reinforce staff for regularly communicating with families about student successes.** This can be accomplished with a brief email, voice mail message, or note home. Positive feedback from staff helps parents feel that teachers are working with them to help their child develop skills to succeed.

- **Encourage staff to use the "communication sandwich."** This means beginning and ending verbal and written communication with a focus on the positive and addressing the problem or difficulty in the middle (Lavoie, 2008).

- **Nurture communication that helps families know that you appreciate their child as an individual.** Communication should include relaying specific information or events that indicate that you have personal knowledge about the student.

- **Remind staff that it is best to avoid telling parents about minor problems that they already know about.** It is not the parents' job to fix every problem involving their child that occurs at school, and they are usually well aware that there are difficulties.

- **Appoint a primary contact.** Consider appointing a member of your staff (e.g., assistant principal, school counselor) as the primary contact for a family. This can greatly alleviate teacher, staff, and parent stress levels because the point of contact is consistent.

- **Relieve staff members who support families from specific duties.** Recognize that the staff member may have to devote considerable time to interacting with the family and, therefore, may need to be relieved of other duties to be able to do everything well and not burn out.

Summary

Effective communication with families is one of the most important ways to help them feel that school personnel understand their concerns and sincerely care about their child. Strengthening your staff's ability to listen empathically, use communication techniques that validate parental concerns, and "sandwich" positive and negative feedback will positively impact the relationship between families and school personnel and, ultimately, benefit students' lives.

CHAPTER 4

Strategies for Working With School Staff

■ ■ ■

B ecause HF-ASD is a complex disorder, your staff will benefit greatly from the support of the administration because administrators set the tone for the building. The administrator who respects staff will, in turn, receive respect. The administrator who displays acceptance of students with HF-ASD will have staff who demonstrate similar behaviors.

Strategies for Supporting School Staff

The following initiatives by administrators may be helpful for staff members:

- **Provide time for team members to meet**. Allowing the team to meet regularly gives them an opportunity to support one another, collaborate and brainstorm on challenges they are facing, and develop coordinated approaches.

- **Support your staff in using *The Underlying Characteristics Checklist*** (UCC; Aspy & Grossman, 2007). The UCC is key to understanding the student's strengths and concerns. Once the

UCC is completed by both school staff and family members, interventions can be matched to the student's ASD. This is essential to school (and life) success (Grossman & Aspy, 2007). For a sample, please see page 33.

- **Protect the student with HF-ASD from problem peers**. Students with HF-ASD are vulnerable. They are naïve, have poor social judgment, and are frequently targeted by their peers. Therefore, to a great extent we want to protect them from poor social models.

- **Build a network of social supports**. Assign a staff member, such as a speech pathologist, occupational therapist, counselor, inclusion specialist, psychologist, or other professionals, to build a network of social supports for students with HF-ASD, who generally benefit from belonging to a small group of friends who look after each other. Developing a group of friends often makes the difference between success and failure for students with HF-ASD. It is important facilitate the development of these groups because developing a social network like this does not come naturally to them. If the Circle of Friends or Lunch Bunch concept is used, it is recommended that more than two neurotypical students be involved. Students making up the group should be (a) high-status peers, (b) generally compliant with school rules, (c) socially astute, and (d) genuinely interested in (and, hopefully, like) the student with HF-ASD.

- **Create a home base**. A home base is a place in the school where the student can go to (a) plan or review the day's events, (b) escape the stress of the classroom, (c) prevent a meltdown, or (d) regain control if a meltdown has occurred. The location is not important – the counselor's office, speech-language pathologist's room, or resource room can all serve as a home base. It is essential that the home base is viewed as a positive environment. Home base is not timeout! Nor is it not an escape from classroom tasks. Student take their class work to home base. Some students need home base to be scheduled as a regular part of their day. For example, a home base at the beginning of the day can serve to preview the day's schedule, introduce and get familiar with changes in the typical routine, ensure that the student's materials are organized, or prime for specific subjects. Home base can also be scheduled after particularly stressful activities or classes to gain a little respite and de-stress before going on to complete the rest of the day.

- **Identify a safe person**. Perhaps one of the most important ways to build in supports is to identify a "safe person," one who knows the student and can help in the event that the student becomes overwhelmed or confused. This person functions as an unobtrusive facilitator and a social interpreter to help the student with social, communication, and academic skills. This individual also serves as a resource for other staff members and as a liaison with the family. In middle or high school, it is often helpful to create a team of "safe people" who can provide social/emotional supports throughout the day.

- **Have alternative arrangements** for the student when there is a substitute teacher. This may include allowing the student to spend the day with a familiar teacher or alerting the parent in advance of a substitute teacher so that the student is prepared.

- **Provide training.** It is essential that educational professionals understand how to use teaching strategies and supports specifically designed for learners on the autism spectrum. Three sets of evidence-based practices in ASD have been identified by the National Autism Center (NAC; 2015), the National Professional Developmental Center on Autism Spectrum Disorder (NPDC; 2015), and the Centers for Medicare and Medicaid Services (CMS; 2010). While the NAC, NPDC, and CMS conducted their reviews independently using different criteria, the outcomes of each are remarkably similar, lending validity to the identified practices. However, because of differences in terminology and criteria, the terms used to describe practices sometimes differ across the three centers (e.g., social narratives vs. story-based intervention package). The practices identified by the three organizations are divided into categories. For example, "antecedent-based interventions" refer globally to interventions that precede the occurrence of an interfering behavior and lead to the reduction of the behavior. This category includes interventions such as (a) social scripts, (b) home base, and (c) video modeling. Free training modules on evidence-based practices may be found at www.autisminternetmodules.org and http://autismpdc.fpg.unc.edu.

- **Support school transitions.** Everyone must adjust to new environments at various points of their lives. Adjustments may involve adapting to a new school year, a new school, a new teacher, or other things or events that are different than what we are used to. Transitions can be particularly challenging for individuals with HF-ASD, as they often experience considerable anxiety when faced with new situations. Moreover, many have difficulty understanding the expectations and routines in new environments without direct instruction. The Transition Checklist in Appendix D can guide this process. In addition to guiding the transition process, this instrument allows educators and family members to consider the interventions that would best support the learner.

- **Consider the role of homework in the life of the student with HF-ASD.** It is generally agreed that the purpose of homework is for students to practice information they already know in order to become fluent and automatic (Grodner & Rupp, 2013). Many students with HF-ASD arrive home from school exhausted and overwhelmed. Often they "hold it all together" at school, only to experience a meltdown once they get home. Homework can add to this stress with its demands time and academic demands time. Students with HF-ASD need their evenings to de-stress to prepare for the next day. Thus, teachers must consider the impact of homework on the students and their families.

- **Match teachers and students.** Most students with HF-ASD do well with structured, yet flexible teachers, so it may be appropriate to personally select the teachers for these students. In spite of best efforts, however, sometimes a match between teacher and student does not exist. In such situations, an administrator may end up struggling to provide a balance between allowing a teacher to adapt and change to meet the needs of a student or change teachers mid-year. Use your discretion, but carefully matching teachers and students can sometimes save everyone on the team time and energy.

Summary

Remember that students with HF-ASD are, first and foremost, students. Look for the similarities rather than the differences between students with HF-ASD and the rest of the student body. Unfortunately, human beings are hardwired to be critical and to look for differences. It is imperative that we see the similarities among all people in order to develop empathy. Without empathy, it is almost impossible to develop positive relationships. Friendships and other meaningful relationships require empathy skills, such as listening, understanding verbal and nonverbal cues, and learning and appreciating the differences in others.

These strategies outlined in this chapter will help your staff feel supported in numerous ways. A supportive administrator can help combat the high levels of teacher stress and burnout (Scheuermann, Webber, Boutot, & Goodwin, 2013). In addition, the strategies will help build the capacity of your school to effectively work with students with HF-ASD!

References

■ ■ ■

Agency for Healthcare Research and Quality. (2016). *Patient and family engagement in primary care*. Retrieved from http://www.ahrq.gov/professionals/quality-patient-safety/patient-fam...

American Psychiatric Association. (2013). *Diagnostic and statistical manual of mental disorders* (5th ed.). Arlington, VA: American Psychiatric Publishing.

Applefield, A. E. (2015, May 24). *Asperger's bullying*. Retrieved from https://ariaeappleford.com/2015/05/24/bullying-aspergers/_.

Ashwin, C., Chapman, E., Howells, J., Rhydderch, D., Walker, I., & Baron-Cohen, S. (2014). Enhanced olfactory sensitivity in autism spectrum conditions. *Molecular Autism, 5*(1), 1.

Aspy, R., & Grossman, B. G. (2007). *The Underlying Characteristics Checklist-High Functioning (UCC-HF)*.

Aspy, R., & Grossman, B. G. (2011). *The Ziggurat Model: A framework for designing comprehensive interventions for individuals with high-functioning autism and Asperger syndrome* (2nd ed.).

Aspy, R., Grossman, B. G., Myles, B. S., & Henry, S. A. (2016). *FBA to Z: Functional behavior and interventions plans for individuals with ASD*.

Autism Topics. (n.d.). *Autism – Strengths*. Retrieved from autismtopics.org.

Baker, A.E.Z., Lane, A., Angley, M. T., & Young, R. L. (2008). The relationship between sensory processing patterns and behavioral responsiveness in autistic disorder: A pilot study. *Journal of Autism and Developmental Disorders, 38,* 867-875.

Barnhill, G. P. (2004). Asperger syndrome: A guide for secondary school principals. *Principal Leadership Magazine, 5*(3), 11-15.

Bennetto, L., Kuschner, E. S., & Hyman, S. L. (2007). Olfaction and taste processing in autism. *Biological Psychiatry, 62*(9), 1015-1021.

Bethune, L. K., & Test, D. W. (2014, September). *Characteristics of evidence-based predictors of post-school success.* Presentation at Reaching the Summit Conference, Greensboro, NC.

Butler, J. (2015). *How safe is the schoolhouse? An analysis of state seclusion and restraint laws and policies.* Retrieved from http://www.autcom.org/pdf/HowSafeSchoolhouse.pdf

Centers for Disease Control and Prevention. (2014). *Autism spectrum disorders.* Retrieved from http://www.cdc.gov/ncbddd/autism/data.html

Centers for Medicare and Medicaid Services. (2010). *Autism spectrum disorders: Final report on environmental scan.* Washington, DC: Author.

Chiang, H. M., Cheung, Y. K., Hickson, L., Xiang, R., & Tsai, L. Y. (2012). Predictive factors of participation in postsecondary education for high school leavers with autism. *Journal of Autism and Developmental Disorders, 42*(5), 685-696.

Council for Exceptional Children's Division of Career Development and Transition Publications Committee (DCDT). (2014, July). *Fast facts: Student support.* Retrieved from http://higherlogicdownload.s3.amazonaws.com/SPED/7deb9f2e-5efb-494a-

86f6-51e993a1d062/UploadedImages/Fast%20Fact_Student%20Support_Final.pdf

DeLoache, J. S., Simcock, G., & Macari, S. (2007). Planes, trains, automobiles — and tea sets: Extremely intense interests in very young children. *Developmental Psychology, 43,* 1579-1586.

Ernsperger, L. (2016). *Recognize, respond, report: Preventing and addressing bullying of students with special needs.* Baltimore, MD: Brookes Publishing.

Fiene, L., & Brownlow, C. (2015). Investigating interoception and body awareness in adults with and without autism spectrum disorder. *Autism Research, 8*(6), 709-716.

Fournier, K. A., Hass, C. J., Naik, S. K., Lodha, N., & Cauraugh, J. H. (2010). Motor coordination in autism spectrum disorders: A synthesis and meta-analysis. *Journal of Autism and Developmental Disorders, 40*(10), 1227-1240.

Gomot, M., & Wicker, B. (2012). A challenging, unpredictable world for people with autism spectrum disorder. *International Journal of Psychophysiology, 83*(2), 240-247.

Green, S. A., Hernandez, L., Tottenham, N., Krasileva, K., Bookheimer, S. Y., & Dapretto, M. (2015). Neurobiology of sensory overresponsivity in youth with autism spectrum disorders. *JAMA Psychiatry, 72*(8), 778-786.

Green, S. A., Rudie, J. D., Colich, N. L., Wood, J. J., Shirinyan, D., Hernandez, L., ... & Bookheimer, S. Y. (2013). Overreactive brain responses to sensory stimuli in youth with autism spectrum disorders. *Journal of the American Academy of Child & Adolescent Psychiatry, 52*(11), 1158-1172.

Grodner, A., & Rupp, N. G. (2013). The role of homework in student learning outcomes: Evidence from a field experiment. *The Journal of Economic Education, 44*(2), 93-109.

Heinrichs, B. (2005). *Perfect targets: Asperger syndrome and bullying: Practical solutions for surviving the social world.*

Hudson, J., & Myles, B. S. (2007). *Starting points: How to understand and support children and youth with Asperger syndrome.*

Humphrey, N., & Hebron, J. (2015). Bullying of children and adolescents with autism spectrum conditions: A 'state of the field' review. *International Journal of Inclusive Education, 19*(8), 845-862.

Individuals with Disabilities Education Act, 20 U.S.C. § 1400 (2004).

Ingersoll, B., & Weiner, A. (2013). The broader autism phenotype. In F. R. Volkmar, S. J. Rogers, R. Paul, & K. A. Pelphrey (Eds.), *Handbook of autism and pervasive developmental disorders: Volume 1: Diagnosis, development, and brain mechanisms* (pp. 28-56). Hoboken, NJ: John Wiley and Sons.

Institute of Education Sciences National Center on Statistics. (2016). *Indicators of school crime and safety: 2015.* Washington, DC: U.S. Department of Education, U.S. Department of Justice Office of Justice Programs.

Interactive Research Network. (2014). *IAN research report: Bullying and children with ASD.* Retrieved from https://iancommunity. org/cs/ian_research_reports/ian_research_report_bullying

Jones, D. E., Greenberg, M., & Crowley, M. (2015). Early social-emotional functioning and public health: The relationship between kindergarten social competence and future wellness. *American Journal of Public Health, 105*(11), 2283-2290.

Jones, V. F., & Jones, L. S. (1995). *Comprehensive classroom management: Creating positive learning environments for all students* (4th ed.). Boston, MA: Allyn and Bacon.

Jordan, C. J., & Caldwell-Harris, C. L. (2012). Understanding differences in neurotypical and autism spectrum special interests through Internet forums. *Intellectual and Developmental Disabilities, 50*(5), 391-402.

Kim, Y. S., & Leventhal, B. L. (2015). Genetic epidemiology and insights into interactive genetic and environmental effects in autism spectrum disorders. *Biological Psychiatry, 77*(1), 66-74.

Kushki, A., Chau, T., & Anagnostou, E. (2011). Handwriting difficulties in children with autism spectrum disorders: A scoping review. *Journal of autism and developmental disorders, 41*(12), 1706-1716.

Lavoie, R. (2008). The teacher's role in home/school communication: Everybody wins. *LD Online.* Retrieved from www.ldonline.org/article/28021/.

McGuire, K., Fung, L. K., Hagopian, L., Vasa, R. A., Mahajan, R., Bernal, P., ... & Veenstra-VanderWeele, J. (2016). Irritability and problem behavior in autism spectrum disorder: A practice pathway for pediatric primary care. *Pediatrics, 137*(Supplement 2), S136-S148.

Maïano, C., Normand, C. L., Salvas, M. C., Moullec, G., & Aimé, A. (2016). Prevalence of school bullying among youth with autism spectrum disorders: A systematic review and meta-analysis. *Autism Research, 9,* 610-615.

Marko, M. K., Crocetti, D., Hulst, T., Donchin, O., Shadmehr, R., &

Mostofsky, S. H. (2015). Behavioural and neural basis of anomalous motor learning in children with autism. *Brain, 138*(3), 784-797.

Massachusetts Advocates for Children. (2009). *Targeted, taunted, tormented: The bullying of children with autism spectrum disorder.* Retrieved from http://massadvocates.org/wp-content/uploads/2014/02/Bullying-report1.pdf

Massachusetts Department of Education. (2007). *Discipline of special education students under IDEA 2004.* Retrieved from http://www.doe.mass.edu/sped/IDEA2004/spr_meetings/disc_chart.pdf

Mazurek, M. O., Kanne, S. M., & Wodka, E. L. (2013). Physical aggression in children and adolescents with autism spectrum disorders. *Research in Autism Spectrum Disorders, 7*(3), 455-465.

Memari, A. H., Panahi, N., Fanjar, E., Moshayedi, P., Shafiei, M., Kordi, R., & Ziaee, V. (2015). Children with autism spectrum disorder and patterns of participation in daily physical and play activities. *Neurology Research International.* doi:10.1155./2015/531906

Miodovnik, A., Harstad, E., Sideridis, G., & Huntington, N. (2015). Timing of the diagnosis of attention-deficit/hyperactivity disorder and autism spectrum disorder. *Pediatrics, 136*(4), e830-e837.

Myles, B. S., & Adreon, D. (2001). *Asperger syndrome and adolescence: Practical solutions for school success.*

Myles, B. S., & Aspy, G. (2016). *High-functioning autism and difficult moments: Practical solutions for reducing meltdowns.*

Myles, B. S., Hagen, K., Holverstott, J., Hubbard, A., Adreon, D., & Trautman, M. (2005). *Life journey through autism: An educator's guide to Asperger Syndrome.* Arlington, VA: Organization for

Autism Research.

Myles, B. S., Huggins, A., Rome-Lake, M., Hagiwara, T., Barnhill, G. P., & Griswold, D. E. (2003). Written language profile of children and youth with Asperger Syndrome. *Education and Training in Developmental Disabilities, 38*(4), 362-370.

Myles, B. S., Mahler, K., & Robbins, L. A. (2014). *Sensory issues and high-functioning autism: Practical solutions for making sense of the world* (2nd ed.).

National Autism Center. (2015). *Findings and conclusions: National standards project, Phase 2: Addressing the need for evidence-based practice guidelines for autism spectrum disorder.* Randolph, MA: Author.

National Education Association. (n.d.). *Health and student services: ESPs and bullying prevention: Bullied students confide in nurses, family and community service workers.* Retrieved from http://www.nea.org/home/63932.htm

National Professional Development Center on Autism Spectrum Disorder. (2015). *Evidence-based practice briefs.* Retrieved from http://autismpdc.fpg.unc.edu/content/briefs

National Technical Assistance Center on Transition. (n.d.). *Evidence-based practices and predictors.* Retrieved from http://transitionta.org/effectivepractices

Ohio Employment First. (n.d.). *Evidence-based predictors for post-school success.* Retrieved from http://www.ohioemploymentfirst.org/up_doc/Evidence_Based_Predictors_for_Post_school_Success3_25_15.pdf

Osbourne, A. G., & Russo, C. J. (2009). *Discipline in special education.* Thousand Oaks, CA: Corwin.

Richey, J. A., Damiano, C. R., Sabatino, A., Rittenberg, A., Petty, C., Bizzell, J., ... Dichter, G. S. (2015). Neural mechanisms of emotion regulation in autism spectrum disorder. *Journal of Autism and Developmental Disorders, 45*(11), 3409-3423.

Rowe, D. A., Alverson, C. Y., Unruh, D. K., Fowler, C. H., Kellems, R., & Test, D. W. (2015). A Delphi study to operationalize evidence-based predictors in secondary transition. *Career Development and Transition for Exceptional Individuals, 38*(2), 113-126.

Salazar, F., Baird, G., Chandler, S., Tseng, E., O'Sullivan, T., Howlin, P., Pickles, A., & Simonoff, E. (2015). Co-occurring psychiatric disorders in preschool and elementary school-aged children with autism spectrum disorder. *Journal of Autism and Developmental Disorders, 45,* 2283-2294.

Scheuermann, B., Webber, J., Boutot, E. A., & Goodwin, M. (2003). Problems with personnel preparation in autism spectrum disorders. *Focus on Autism and Other Developmental Disabilities, 18*(3), 197-206.

Shanker, S. (2014). *Broader measures for success: Social/emotional learning: Measuring what matters.* Toronto, Canada: People for Education.

Silberman, S. (2015). *Neurotribes: The legacy of autism and the future of neurodiversity.* New York, NY: Penguin Random House.

Soulières, I., Dawson, M., Samson, F., Barbeau, E. B., Sahyoun, C. P., Strangman, G. E., ... & Mottron, L. (2009). Enhanced visual processing contributes to matrix reasoning in autism. *Human Brain Mapping, 30*(12), 4082-4107.

Sumner, E., Leonard, H. C., & Hill, E. L. (2016). Overlapping phenotypes in autism spectrum disorder and developmental coordination disorder: A cross-syndrome comparison of motor and social skills. *Journal of Autism and Developmental Disorders, 46,* 1-12.

U.S. Department of Education. (2012). *Restraint and seclusion: Resource document.* Washington, DC: Author.

U.S. Department of Education Office for Civil Rights. (2014). *Dear colleague: Bullying.* Washington, DC: Author.

Volkmar, F., R., Klin, A., Schultz, R. T., Rubin, E., & Bronen, R. (2000). Asperger's disorder. *American Journal of Psychiatry, 157*(2), 262-267.

Wehman, P., Schall, C., Carr, S., Targett, P., West, M., & Cifu, G., (2014). Transition from school to adulthood for youth with autism spectrum disorder: What we know and what we need to know. *Journal of Disability Policy Studies, 1,* 30-40.

Whyte, E. M., Nelson, K. E., & Khan, K. S. (2013). Learning of idiomatic language expressions in a group intervention for children with autism. *Autism, 17*(4), 449-464.

Winter-Messiers, M. A. (2014). Harnessing the power of special interest areas in the classroom. In K. D. Buron & P. Wolfberg (Eds.), *Learners on the autism spectrum: Preparing highly qualified educators and related practitioners* (pp. 288-313).

Appendix A

Modified Inventory of Wrongful Activities

Rebecca Heinrichs

From Heinrichs, R. (2003). *Perfect targets: Asperger syndrome and bullying: Practical solutions for surviving the social world.* Used with permission.

Name: _____ Grade: _____

Date:_____

Gender: (circle or underline) Male   Female

School: (circle or underline)   Public   Private   Home school

Has a student (or students) from your school done any of the following things to you?

CHECK ALL ITEMS that have happened to you THIS SCHOOL YEAR.

Someone has:

☐ 1. Pulled my hair, hit, pinched, kicked, tripped, bit or spit on me

☐ 2. Torn my clothes or broken my things (such as pencil breaking)

☐ 3. Stolen from me

☐ 4. Scared me or threatened me with a weapon (like a knife or gun)

☐ 5. Said bad things about me (calling me names like "fat" or "freak")

☐ 6. Said bad things about my family (like calling my Dad a "wimp")

Someone has:

☐ 7. Written mean notes about me

☐ 8. Made me afraid to talk in class or make mistakes because of teasing.

☐ 9. Asked me to do things that I get in trouble for doing (like saying something rude to the teacher)

☐ 10. Scared or threatened me into doing something I didn't want to do (like giving up money or doing someone else's home-work)

☐ 11. Asked me to do things that make me uncomfortable (like telling me not to talk to certain people)

☐ 12. Made it hard for me to learn in school because I feel scared, angry, sad, or upset about the way people treat me

Someone has:

☐ 13. Made me not want to go to school because I feel scared, angry, sad, or upset, about the way people treat me

☐ 14. Left me out of a group or activity

☐ 15. Made mean faces at me (like rolling eyes)

☐ 16. Laughed at me to be mean

☐ 17. Used hand signals to be mean (like making an "L" with their fingers and putting it on their forehead)

☐ 18. Made fun of something they think is different about me (like being tall, short, wearing glasses, braces, or talking or walking differently)

Someone has:

☐ 19. Insulted me because I am in a different class or program

☐ 20. Insulted me or made jokes about my color or race

☐ 21. Insulted my ability to learn in class

☐ 22. Made fun of my clothes or my parents' car, house, or job

☐ 23. Insulted me with sexual talk or jokes (could include hand signals like raising the middle finger or name-calling like "slut" or "fag")

☐ 24. Spread sexual rumors about me (like telling people I am "gay" or "easy")

Someone has:

☐ 25. Made me uncomfortable by taking off their clothes or "mooning" me ("mooning" is when someone exposes their bare buttocks to another person)

☐ 26. Pulled (or tried to pull) my clothes off or down

☐ 27. Grabbed, pinched, or kicked me in a private area

☐ 28. Touched me in a sexual way without my permission (like kissing, hugging, putting hands on my private areas or holding me)

☐ 29. Written sexual insults about me on walls, desks, or something else

The next three statements ask your feelings about your teachers and their actions.

CHECK ALL ITEMS that are TRUE for you.

- ☐ 30. I feel some teachers don't like me as well as other students
- ☐ 31. I feel hurt or angry (once a week or more) about a teacher's actions or words
- ☐ 32. I wish my teachers would stop someone who is acting mean to me

CHECK ALL ITEMS that are TRUE for you.

When are mean things said or done to you?

- ☐ 33. Before school
- ☐ 34. Between classes
- ☐ 35. After school
- ☐ 36. During classes
- ☐ 37. At lunch time
- ☐ 38. At after-school activities

CHECK ALL ITEMS that are TRUE for you.

What places should adults watch better to keep students from being mean to you?

- ☐ 39. Hallways
- ☐ 40. Bathrooms
- ☐ 41. Classrooms
- ☐ 42. Lunchrooms
- ☐ 43. Gym lockers
- ☐ 44. Outside on school property

Choose ONLY ONE answer for these questions and WRITE THE LETTER on the line.

___45. Do people act mean to you on the school bus?

    A. I do not ride the school bus

    B. People do not act mean to me on the school bus ride

    C. People act mean to me on the school bus ride

___46. What do most of your teachers do when they see students acting mean?

A. They usually do nothing. They ignore it.

B. They do very little. They might say, "Quit that."

C. They make them stop and teach them not to act that way anymore.

___47. What do you do when you see students acting mean to other students?

A. I sometimes join in and act mean too.

B. I do nothing. I ignore it.

C. I ask people to stop acting mean. I try to stop it.

D. I tell a teacher so he or she can help.

___48. What do you do when people are mean to you at school?

A. I act mean right back.

B. I do nothing. I ignore it or accept it.

C. I tell them to stop.

D. I tell a teacher so he or she can help.

___49. How often are people mean to you at school?

A. Almost never

B. Several times a week

C. About once a day

D. More than once a day

___50. How often do you tell adults at school when people are mean to you?

A. I almost never tell

B. I tell some of the time

C. I tell most of the time

D. I tell every time

___51. What usually happens when you tell an adult at school about someone being mean to you?

    A. It helps a lot

    B. It helps some

    C. It does not make a difference

    D. It makes things worse

___52. What usually happens when you tell your parents about someone being mean to you?

    A. It helps a lot

    B. It helps some

    C. It does not make a difference

    D. It makes things worse

CHECK ALL ITEMS that are TRUE for you.

Which adults at school do you go to for help when someone is being mean to you?

- ☐ 53. Counselor
- ☐ 54. Teacher
- ☐ 55. School psychologist
- ☐ 56. Principal
- ☐ 57. Vice principal
- ☐ 58. Resource teacher
- ☐ 59. Paraprofessional/aide
- ☐ 60. Resource police officer
- ☐ 61. Other

Please include any additional comments here:

Appendix B:

Ziggurat Functional Behavior Assessment and Behavior Intervention Plan

■ ■ ■

Ziggurat FBA/BIP

Luisa's team completed UCC-HF and an ABC-Iceberg that targeted her meltdown behaviors. The Ziggurat Worksheet and CAPS concluded the process.

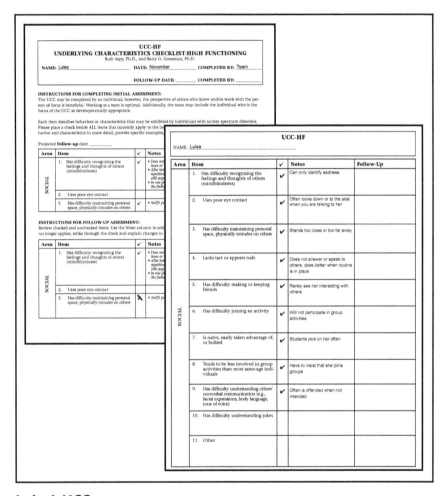

Luisa's UCC.

From Aspy, R., Grossman, B. G., Myles, B. S., & Henry, S. A. (2016). *FBA to Z: Functional behavior and interventions plans for individuals with ASD.*

ABC-Iceberg

Antecedent(s) ———► Behavior ———►Consequence(s)

Antecedent(s)	Behavior	Consequence(s)
• Change in expectation • Loud sounds • Peer teasing • Peers not following rules • Mistakes • Asked to transition from a preferred task • Removal of books	👁 Stomps 👁 Screams 👁 Whines 👁 Runs away, covers head with hood 👁 Swipes at others with arm and hand 👁 Withdraws, then rages	• Teacher redirection • Wait time • ISS • Office referral

Specific Behaviors

Underlying Characteristics

- Difficulty understanding the thoughts and feelings of others
- Naïve, easily taken advantage of, or bullied
- Has problems handling transition and change
- Has strong need for closure or difficulty stopping a task before it is completed
- Has eccentric or intense preoccupations
- Difficulty identifying, quantifying, expressing and/or controlling emotions (only recognizes/expresses in extremes)

- Unmotivated by customary rewards
- Difficulty asking for help
- Withdraws into complex inner worlds/fantasizes often (fascinated with objects)
- Difficulty tolerating mistakes
- Responds in an unusual manner to sounds (withdraws/becomes hyper or aggressive)
- Knows facts and details but has difficulty with abstract reasoning (weak central coherence)

Luisa's ABC-Iceberg with meltdowns.

From Aspy, R., Grossman, B. G., Myles, B. S., & Henry, S. A. (2016). *FBA to Z: Functional behavior and interventions plans for individuals with ASD.*

Ziggurat Worksheet: Functional Behavior Assessment

Name: _____   Date: 1/7

[1] Difficulty understanding of thoughts and feelings of others
[7] Naïve, easily taken advantage or bullied
[14] Eccentric or intense preoccupations
[16] Unmotivated by customary rewards
[18] Problems handling transition and change
[19] Strong need for closure or difficulty stopping a task before it is competed
[29] Difficulty asking for help
[41] Responds in an unusual manner to sounds
[54] Withdraws into complex inner worlds/fantasizes often
[84] Difficulty tolerating mistakes
[87] Difficulty identifying, quantifying, expressing and/or controlling emotions (only understands and expresses in extremes)

*Interventions occur at 3 points:

Prevent – Antecedent before

Teach – Behavior during

Reinforce – Consequence after

Underlying Characteristics *List 1 UCC per row*	Interventions	Ziggurat Levels	*Check All That Apply		
			P	T	R
		Skills to Teach / Obstacle Removal / Structure and Visual/Tactile Supports / Reinforcement / Sensory Differences and Biological Needs	☑	☑	☐
[1] Difficulty understanding thoughts and feelings of others	• Narrate interactions describing the thoughts and feelings of others and how to recognize those feelings. Use movies, videos of Luisa. • Describe Luisa's emotional expressions to her. • Use drawings, photos, stories, videos, role-play, and coaching to teach basic emotion recognition.	Skills to Teach / Obstacle Removal / Structure and Visual/Tactile Supports / Reinforcement / Sensory Differences and Biological Needs			

From Aspy, R., Grossman, B. G., Myles, B. S., & Henry, S. A. (2016). *FBA to Z: Functional behavior and interventions plans for individuals with ASD.*

Underlying Characteristics *List 1 UCC per row*	Interventions	Ziggurat Levels	*Check All That Apply P T R
[7] Naïve, easily taken advantage of or bullied	• Monitor very closely for bullying or social misunderstandings. • Provide Luisa with a "home base" throughout her day. Adults should permit access at any time when first implemented. • Teach Luisa how to remove herself from conflict in a way that does not involve physical aggression. For example, she may go to her assigned "home base," count to 10, walk away. • Reinforce Luisa for removing herself from conflict using special interests. • Do not ask Luisa to independently resolve conflicts with peers. She does not have the skills and will be overwhelmed by the demands of the task. Assist Luisa to resolve conflicts and teach her the process gradually. • Teach Luisa the warning signs of teasing or bullying. Use role-play, video, and scenarios. • Use "social autopsies" following any bullying episode.	Skills to Teach / Obstacle Removal / Structure and Visual/Tactile Supports / Reinforcement / Sensory Differences and Biological Needs	P ☑ T ☑ R ☑
[14] Eccentric or intense preoccupations	• Luisa requires frequent reinforcement in order for her to learn new skills and maintain those that she has learned. She would benefit from a reinforcement menu. Use her special interests as reinforcers and structure them so they are not disruptive to her school day. Note that Luisa's special interests will evolve; therefore, reinforcers should be updated to ensure that there are always salient choices.	Skills to Teach / Obstacle Removal / Structure and Visual/Tactile Supports / Reinforcement / Sensory Differences and Biological Needs	P ☐ T ☑ R ☑

Underlying Characteristics *List 1 UCC per row*	Interventions	Ziggurat Levels	*Check All That Apply P T R
[16] Unmotivated by customary rewards	• Luisa requires frequent reinforcement in order for her to learn new skills and maintain those that she has learned. She would benefit from a reinforcement menu. Use her special interests as reinforcers and structure them so they are not disruptive to her school day. Note that Luisa's special interests will evolve; therefore, reinforcers should be updated to ensure that there are always salient choices.	Skills to Teach / Obstacle Removal / Structure and Visual/Tactile Supports / Reinforcement / Sensory Differences and Biological Needs	P □ T ☑ R ☑
[18] Problems handling transition and change	• Practice skills for coping with change, reinforce for successful imitation or demonstration of skills. • Prime just before change – remind that it is OK and briefly review coping options. • Sensory diet, built into the daily routine and included in visual schedules. • Parents and staff should recognize that when Luisa is in conflict/distress, she is least able to be flexible. Use few words and provide clear and concise instructions. • Provide Luisa with a "home base" throughout her day. Include her in the selection of appropriate places to ensure that there is a location in each school setting during her day. Adults should permit access at any time when first implemented.	Skills to Teach / Obstacle Removal / Structure and Visual/Tactile Supports / Reinforcement / Sensory Differences and Biological Needs	P ☑ T ☑ R ☑

From Aspy, R., Grossman, B. G., Myles, B. S., & Henry, S. A. (2016). *FBA to Z: Functional behavior and interventions plans for individuals with ASD.*

Underlying Characteristics *List 1 UCC per row*	Interventions	Ziggurat Levels	*Check All That Apply P	T	R
[19] Strong need for closure or difficulty stopping a task before it is completed	• An individualized daily schedule is a critical tool for successful transitioning. Include on the schedule the plan for completing incomplete tasks. • Write start and end times on assignments to make the time needed finite to Luisa and to increase her awareness of what is needed to complete one task; provide incentives for completion within the projected time frame. • Provide a visual timer to assist Luisa in preparing for ending a task. • When given a time-limited preferred task, use a visual timer or write down the stop time. • Try not to give Luisa more work than she can complete in the allotted time. • Reinforce Luisa for starting a task along with her classmates. • Teach Luisa to observe classmates and begin tasks with them. • Teach Luisa to draw a finished line on her paper when time is "up."	Skills to Teach / Obstacle Removal / Structure and Visual/Tactile Supports / Reinforcement / Sensory Differences and Biological Needs	☑	☑	☑
[29] Difficulty asking for help	• Provide visuals or teach Luisa nonverbal ways to ask adults for help when needed. • Provide Luisa opportunities to practice ways to verbally, and appropriately, ask adults for help. • Use 1:1 or small-group opportunities to teach Luisa common times when she might need to ask for help from others throughout her school day and at home.	Skills to Teach / Obstacle Removal / Structure and Visual/Tactile Supports / Reinforcement / Sensory Differences and Biological Needs	☑	☑	☐

From Aspy, R., Grossman, B. G., Myles, B. S., & Henry, S. A. (2016). *FBA to Z: Functional behavior and interventions plans for individuals with ASD.*

Underlying Characteristics *List 1 UCC per row*	Interventions	Ziggurat Levels	*Check All That Apply P T R		

[41] Responds in an unusual manner to sounds	• Luisa has difficulty coping with the noise level in the cafeteria. Possible ways to facilitate success in this setting include:
	  o Use of ear plugs or headphones to dampen noise level
	  o Shortening time in the cafeteria
	  o Use of a calming activity prior to lunch (seek advice of occupational therapist for activities that would be calming to Luisa)
	  o Prime Luisa prior to lunch to remind her of coping skills for this setting (e.g., access to safe place, ear plugs)
	  o Use trained peer buddies during lunchtime
	• Provide reinforcement.
		Skills to Teach / Obstacle Removal / Structure and Visual/Tactile Supports / Reinforcement / Sensory Differences and Biological Needs	☑	☐	☑

[54] Withdraws into complex inner worlds/fantasizes often	• Prior to giving Luisa a task that she often finds to be frustrating, remind her of her calming strategies. • Provide Luisa with a "home base" throughout her day. Include her in the selection of appropriate places to ensure that there is a location in each school setting during her day. Adults should permit access at any time. • Practice skills for coping with change, reinforce for successful imitation or demonstration of skills. • Prime just before change – remind her that it is OK and briefly review coping options. • Use sensory diet, built into the daily routine and included in visual schedules.	Skills to Teach / Obstacle Removal / Structure and Visual/Tactile Supports / Reinforcement / Sensory Differences and Biological Needs	☑	☑	☐

From Aspy, R., Grossman, B. G., Myles, B. S., & Henry, S. A. (2016). *FBA to Z: Functional behavior and interventions plans for individuals with ASD.*

Underlying Characteristics *List 1 UCC per row*	Interventions	Ziggurat Levels	*Check All That Apply P T R
[84] Difficulty tolerating mistakes	• Directly teach and role-play that making mistakes is okay. • Teach Luisa when and how to report concerns about others' behavior (e.g., if you need to report a peer's behavior, do so privately). Teach her how her peers feel when she reports their behavior to an adult. • Give high levels of positive feedback. • If corrections are needed, remind Luisa that everyone needs corrections and it is OK to need them. • Provide a sensory diet.	Skills to Teach / Obstacle Removal / Structure and Visual/ Tactile Supports / Reinforcement / Sensory Differences and Biological Needs	P ☑ T ☑ R ☑
87] Difficulty identifying, quantifying, expressing and/or controlling emotions (only understands and expresses in extremes)	• Use sensory diet, built into the daily routine and included in visual schedules. • Parents and staff should recognize that when Luisa is in conflict/distress, she is least able to be flexible. Use few words and provide clear and concise instructions. • Teach Luisa to recognize her emotions and rate them on an Incredible 5-Point Scale (Buron & Curtis, 2012).	Skills to Teach / Obstacle Removal / Structure and Visual/ Tactile Supports / Reinforcement / Sensory Differences and Biological Needs	P ☑ T ☑ R ☐

From Aspy, R., Grossman, B. G., Myles, B. S., & Henry, S. A. (2016). *FBA to Z: Functional behavior and interventions plans for individuals with ASD.*

Comprehensive Autism Planning System (CAPS)

Individual's Name: Luisa   Date: November   Completed by: _____   Team: _____

Time	Activity	Skills to Teach	Structure and Visual/Tactile Supports + Obstacle Removal (OR)	Reinforcement	Sensory and Biological Strategies (+ OR)	Communication/ Social Skills*	Data Collection	Generalization Plan
8:00-8:40	Home Room	1. How to handle schedule changes • 2. Understanding that everyone makes mistakes • 3. Importance of finishing work • 4. Teach self-regulation using the Incredible 5-Point Scale	• Prime before changes • Provide visual schedule with detail on what to do with unfinished work • Directly teach and role play that mistakes are okay	• Reinforcer menu • Verbal reinforcement	• Home base • Sensory diet • Incredible 5-Point Scale	• Monitor closely for bullying or social misunderstandings • Use few words when Luisa is stressed	• 1, 2, 3, 4.* Rate Luisa on a 5-Point Scale following schedule changes, mistakes, unfinished work • Have Luisa rate herself on the scale	Use the Incredible 5-Point Scale at home

From Aspy, R., Grossman, B. G., Myles, B. S., & Henry, S. A. (2016). *FBA to Z: Functional behavior and interventions plans for individuals with ASD.*

Time	Activity	Skills to Teach	Structure and Visual/ Tactile Supports + Obstacle Removal (OR)	Reinforcement	Sensory and Biological Strategies (+ OR)	Communication/ Social Skills*	Data Collection	Generalization Plan
8:45-9:45	Social Skills Group	• 1. Understanding thoughts and feelings of others and self • 2. Removing self from conflict • 3. Understanding conflicts • 4. Reporting concerns to adults • 5. Asking for help	• Use mindreading software • Narrate interactions describing the thoughts and feelings of others and how to recognize those feelings. Use movies, videos of Luisa • Describe Luisa's emotional expressions to her • Use drawings, photos, stories, videos, role-play and coaching to teach basic emotion recognition • Luisa does not have the skills to resolve conflicts with peers and will be overwhelmed by the demands of the task. Assist Luisa to resolve conflicts and teach her the process gradually using visuals and bullying curriculum.	• Reinforcer menu • Verbal reinforcement	• Home base • Sensory diet • Incredible 5-Point Scale	• Monitor closely for bullying or social misunderstandings • Use few words when Luisa is stressed • Use help card	• 1. (software tracks) • 2, 3, 4. Rate Luisa on a 5-Point Scale following schedule changes, mistakes, unfinished work • Have Luisa rate herself on the scale	• Prime before changes at home • Use the Incredible 5-Point Scale

From Aspy, R., Grossman, B. G., Myles, B. S., & Henry, S. A. (2016). *FBA to Z: Functional behavior and interventions plans for individuals with ASD.*

Time	Activity	Skills to Teach	Structure and Visual/Tactile Supports + Obstacle Removal (OR)	Reinforcement	Sensory and Biological Strategies (+ OR)	Communication/ Social Skills*	Data Collection	Generalization Plan
			• Teach Luisa the warning signs of teasing or bullying. Use role play, video, and scenarios. • Use "social autopsies" following any bullying episode • Prime before changes • Use visual schedule with detail on what to do with unfinished work • Match work to time available • Use visuals to teach Luisa when and how to report concerns about others' behavior ("If you need to report a peer's behavior, do so privately") • Use cartooning to teach her how her peers feel when she reports their behavior to an adult					

Time	Activity	Skills to Teach	Structure and Visual/Tactile Supports + Obstacle Removal (OR)	Reinforcement	Sensory and Biological Strategies (+ OR)	Communication/Social Skills*	Data Collection	Generalization Plan
9:50-10:50 12:35-1:35 2:45-3:45 (social studies, Monday, Wednesday, Friday; science, Tuesday, Thursday)	Literacy Math Social Studies/Science	• Following a visual schedule • Finishing unfinished work • Observing peers • Asking for help • Understanding thoughts and feelings of self	• Prime before changes • Provide visual schedule with detail on what to do with unfinished work • Use a visual timer • Match work to time available • Teach Luisa to observe classmates and completing tasks with them • Teach Luisa to draw a finished line on her paper when time is "up" • Provide Luisa opportunities to practice ways to verbally, and appropriately, ask adults for help • Practice coping with change through role-play and video • Directly teach and role-play that making mistakes is okay	• Reinforcer menu • Verbal reinforcement especially for starting tasks on time)	• Home base • Sensory diet • Incredible 5-Point Scale	• Monitor closely for bullying or social misunderstandings • Use few words when Luisa is stressed • Help card	• 1,2,3,4. • Rate Luisa on a 5-Point Scale following schedule changes, mistakes, unfinished work • Have Luisa rate herself on the scale	

Time	Activity	Skills to Teach	Structure and Visual/ Tactile Supports + Obstacle Removal (OR)	Reinforcement	Sensory and Biological Strategies (+ OR)	Communication/ Social Skills*	Data Collection	Generalization Plan
10:55-11:55	PE	• Understanding thoughts and feelings of self	• Prime before changes • Visual schedule with detail on what to do with unfinished work	• Reinforcer menu • Verbal rein-forcement	• Home base • Sensory diet • Incredible 5-Point Scale	• Monitor very closely for bullying or social misunderstandings • Use few words when Luisa is stressed • Help card	• 1,2,3,4. • Rate Luisa on a 5-Point Scale following schedule changes, mistakes, unfinished work • Have Luisa rate herself on the scale	
1:40-2:40	Recess	• Interact with peer buddy with at least four exchanges	• Prime before changes • Visual schedule	• Reinforcer menu • Verbal rein-forcement	• Home base • Sensory diet • Incredible 5-Point Scale	• Monitor very closely for bullying or social misunderstandings • Use few words when Luisa is stressed • Help card • Use of a calming activity prior to lunch (seek advice of OT) • Peer buddy at recess	• Monday, # of exchang-es	

Time	Activity	Skills to Teach	Structure and Visual/ Tactile Supports + Obstacle Removal (OR)	Reinforcement	Sensory and Biological Strategies (+ OR)	Communication/ Social Skills*	Data Collection	Generalization Plan
12:30	Lunch	• Interact with peer buddy with at least four exchanges	• Prime before changes • Visual schedule with detail on what to do with unfinished work	• Reinforcement menu • Verbal reinforcement	• Home base • Sensory diet • Incredible 5-Point Scale	• Monitor very closely for bullying or social misunderstandings • Use few words when Luisa is stressed • Help card • Use of ear plugs or headphones to dampen noise level • Shorten time in the cafeteria • Prime Luisa prior to lunch to remind her of coping skills for this setting (e.g., access to safe place, ear plugs.) • Use trained peer buddies during lunchtime	• Tuesday, Wednesday, # of exchanges	

* Communication/Social Skills. This column is a reminder that almost all activities include a communication and social component. Supports for communication and social skills can come from the following columns of the Ziggurat Worksheet: Sensory and Biological, Structure and Visual/Tactile Support, Obstacle Removal, and Skills to Teach.

Appendix C:
Student Perspective Analysis

■ ■ ■

Student Perspective Analysis

To the Interviewer:

Gather as much information as possible beforehand. Helpful information may include:

A. The student's daily schedule

B. Teachers' names and the courses they teach

C. Names and roles of other adults the student encounters

D. Recent classroom assignments (it is often helpful to obtain samples of all types of assignments in all subject areas)

If you have no prior information, you may need to break up the interview into several different time periods and assess the whole day.

Discuss the reason for gathering information with the student. The following statement can be used to help the student understand the functional analysis, "The reason I'm asking these questions is so that we can learn about the things that are bothering you at school. Some of these things we may be able to fix. Other things we cannot change. Just because I'm listening to your answers does not mean that I can changes all of these things. It may be helpful for your teachers to know what is bothering you, because this information may help them understand you. When a person learns what is on someone's mind, it provides information about what that person is thinking. This can help people get along and respect each other, even if many things about the situation cannot be changed."

Please note that the form specifically suggests using the name of a school subject or the name of a teacher rather than pronouns. Students with HF-ASD often find pronouns confusing; therefore, the questions will be clearer if you specifically use the teacher's name rather than *he/she* or *they*. Ask questions 1 through 29 about **each** class the student attends. Complete all of the questions for one class or setting before going on to another.

Student Perspective Analysis

School
(NOTE: Ask these questions for each of the student's classes.)

1. What is your first (next) class in school?

2. Who's your teacher?

3. Does <u>teacher's name</u> notice when you do a good job?

4. What does <u>teacher's name</u> do that tells you you've done a good job?

5. Do you think <u>teacher's name</u> likes you?

6. What does <u>teacher's name</u> do to show you he/she likes you?

7. Do you usually work alone or with others?

8. What kinds of things do you do alone?

9. What kinds of things do you do with others?

10. Which do you prefer?

11. Is the work difficult or easy?

12. What is the easy part of the schoolwork?

13. What part of schoolwork don't you like in <u>name class</u> or <u>subject</u>?

14. If you could change one thing about <u>name class or subject,</u> what would that be?

15. Name one easy thing in <u>subject's name</u> class.

16. What is one thing you are good at in <u>subject's name</u> class?

17. Do you have any problems with other students in <u>teacher's name</u> class?

18. Which students do you have problems with?

19. Tell me about the problem(s)?

20. What would help the situation?

21. Do you always sit in the same seat?

22. Do you like where you are sitting? Why or why not?

23. How does <u>teacher's name</u> let you know what the homework is?

24. Does <u>teacher's name</u> make any changes that bother you?

25. Can you think of anything <u>teacher's name</u> does that bothers you? What?

26. Are there any things in the classroom that really bother you a lot? (noises, smell, light, temperature etc.)

27. Do you have enough time to do what <u>teacher's name</u> asks?

28. Do you have enough time to switch activities in name the class?

29. Do you have enough time to get your work done?

30. Rank your classes (including bus, lunch) in order with 1 being the best and __ being the worst. (Give the student a list of all classes and activities to include.)

RANK	CLASSES

31. Rank your teachers and other adults you see at school in order, with 1 being the best and __ being the worst. (Give the student list of teachers and adults to include.)

RANK	TEACHERS' NAMES

Bus (NOTE: You may need to conduct two interviews one for the morning bus and another for the afternoon bus.)

32. Who is your bus driver?

33. Does <u>bus driver's name</u> like you? Dislike you?

34. What does the bus driver do that tells you bus driver likes/ doesn't like you?

35. Where do you sit on the bus?

36. Do you sit near the bus driver? If no, would you like to?

37. Do you sit in the same seat every day?

38. Does anyone sit in the seat next to you? Who?

39. Are there students are on your bus you like? Who?

40. Do you ever talk to them?

41. What do you talk about?

42. What do they talk about?

43. Are there students on the bus you do not like? Who?

44. Why don't you like them?

45. Do you like riding the bus? Why or why not? (If no, question further.)

Lunch

46. What time do you each lunch?

47. Do you always sit in the same seat?

48. Who do you like to sit with at lunch?

49. Is there anyone you do not like to sit with at lunch? Who? Why?

50. Do you have enough time to eat lunch?

51. Do you like lunchtime?

52. Does the noise in the cafeteria bother you?

53. Do the smells in the cafeteria bother you?

54. If you could change one thing about lunchtime, what would it be?

Thanks to Dena Gitlitz for her invaluable assistance in developing this interview form.

Completed Items From Student Perspective Analysis

School
(NOTE: Ask these questions for each of the student's classes.)

1. What is your **first** (next) class in school? **Computer.**

2. Who's your teacher? **Ms. McHale.**

3. Does **Ms. McHale** notice when you do a good job? **How would I know what she notices?**

4. What does **Ms. McHale** do that tells you you've done a good job? **Nothing.**

5. Do you think **Ms. McHale** likes you? **Yes.**

6. What does **Ms. McHale** do to show you she likes you? **She says hi every morning.**

7. Do you usually work alone or with others? **Alone.**

8. What kinds of things do you do alone? **Practice keyboarding, using Microsoft Excel, or developing a PowerPoint.**

9. What kinds of things do you do with others? **I always work alone in this class.**

10. Which do you prefer? **I like working alone.**

11. Is the work difficult or easy? **Moderate.**

12. What is the easy part of the schoolwork? **All of it is fairly easy.**

13. What part of schoolwork don't you like in **Ms. McHale's computer class**? **Practicing keyboarding. It is boring, and I am not very fast.**

14. If you could change one thing about **computer class**, what would that be? **We would just work on interesting things like developing PowerPoints on subjects we like or learning how to build a website.**

15. Name one easy thing in **computer class**. **I don't know.**

16. What is one thing you are good at in **computer class**? **Putting interesting graphics in my PowerPoint presentations.**

17. Do you have any problems with other students in **Ms. McHale's** class? **No.**

18. Which students do you have problems with? **No problems. (*The interviewer did not ask questions 18-20 because the student indicated that he is not having problems with other students in this class.*)**

19. Tell me about the problem(s)?

20. What would help the situation?

21. Do you always sit in the same seat? **Yes.**

22. Do you like where you are sitting? Why or why not? **Yes, but I'd like more games on my computer. Also, I have to move away from my seat to copy from the board. I cannot see the board from my seat.**

23. How does **Mrs. McHale** let you know what the homework is? **We don't have homework in this class.**

24. Does **Mrs. McHale** make any changes that bother you? **No.**

25. Can you think of anything **Mrs. McHale** does that bothers you? **Sometimes she touches my shoulder.**

26. Are there any things in the classroom that really bother you a lot? (noises, smell, light, temperature, etc.) **No.**

27. Do you have enough time to do what **Mrs. McHale** asks? **I guess so. There's always more that I want to add to my PowerPoint presentations.**

28. Do you have enough time to switch activities in **computer class**? **Yes.**

29. Do you have enough time to get your work done? **Yes, except my PowerPoint presentations.**

2nd Class

1. What is your **next class** in school? **Math.**

2. Who's your teacher? **Mr. Greenfield.**

3. Does **Mr. Greenfield** notice when you do a good job? **Yes.**

4. What does **Mr. Greenfield** do that tells you you've done a good job? **He writes something on my paper or tells me I did a good job**

5. Do you think **Mr. Greenfield** likes you? **I don't know. (*This student relies on very concrete words or interactions to understand teachers. It will be important to instruct school personnel on the importance of providing concrete to the student throughout each class period.*)**

6. What does **Mr. Greenfield** do to show you **he** likes you? **I don't know.**

7. Do you usually work alone or with others? **Sometimes alone, sometimes with others. (*The next few questions were not asked. In general, the interviewer probes about various aspects of class to obtain clues about issues. Often, it is not necessary to ask every question.*)**

8. What kinds of things do you do alone?

9. What kinds of things do you do with others?

10. Which do you prefer?

11. Is the work difficult or easy? **Moderate. The hardest thing is division.**

12. What is the easy part of the schoolwork?

13. What part of schoolwork don't you like in **math**?

14. If you could change one thing about **math class**, what would that be?

15. Name one easy thing in **math.**

16. What is one thing you are good at in **math** class?

17. Do you have any problems with other students in **Mr. Greenfield's** class?

18. Which students do you have problems with? **Usually with two people. I would like to work with Colin. I've worked with Nathan. That was a problem. Nathan was annoying. He called me names and kicked me under the table. I also don't like the sound of his voice – it is whiny. Now Mr. Towerman has moved him away from me. I don't like working with Scott either. (*School personnel need to carefully monitor this situation and ensure that these students are not in the same area without close supervision.*)**

19. Tell me about the problem(s)? (*The student elaborated on question 18, so questions 19 & 20 were not asked.*)

20. What would help the situation?

21. Do you always sit in the same seat? **We switched two times. The first time couldn't be helped because we moved to a different classroom. Now I work alone. I'm kind of sad because I moved away from my friend, Collin. It's annoying that other students can help each other and I can't have that.**

22. Do you like where you are sitting? Why or why not? **It's ok, but there are lots of bugs.**

23. How does **Mr. Greenfield** let you know what the homework is? (*The student did not answer, so the interviewer made a note to check on how Mr. Greenfield informs students about homework assignments.*)

24. Does **Mr. Greenfield** make any changes that bother you? **No.**

25. Can you think of anything **Mr. Greenfield** does that bothers you? **No.**

26. Are there any things in the classroom that really bother you a lot? (noises, smell, light, temperature, etc.) **No.**

27. Do you have enough time to do what **Mr. Greenfield** asks? (*The next questions were not asked by the interviewer because the student did not seem distraught about things happening in this class.*)

28. Do you have enough time to switch activities in **math**?

29. Do you have enough time to get your work done?

3rd Class

1. What is your first **(next)** class in school? **Science.**

2. Who's your teacher? **Mr. Towerman.**

3. Does <u>**Mr. Towerman**</u> notice when you do a good job? **Usually.**

4. What does <u>**Mr. Towerman**</u> do that tells you you've done a good job? **By telling me my grade.**

5. Do you think <u>**Mr. Towerman**</u> likes you? **I heard he would like me to move to a different class. Does this count?**

6. What does **Mr. Towerman** do to show you he likes you? **I don't know.**

7. Do you usually work alone or with others? **In a group.**

8. What kinds of things do you do alone? (***This question was not asked due to the answer to question #7.***)

9. What kinds of things do you do with others? **Experiments and projects.**

10. Which do you prefer? **I'd like it better if I could work alone.**

11. Is the work difficult or easy? **Difficult.** What's difficult? **The science project.** Why? **Because I am behind. I forgot to tell my dad. Actually, I thought if I gave Dad the paper about the science project, he would be mad that I am behind, so I didn't give it to him at all.** (***The interviewer should address home-school communication.***)

12. What is the easy part of the schoolwork? **None of it.**

13. What part of schoolwork don't you like in <u>**science class**</u>? **It's too much work.**

14. If you could change one thing about <u>**science class**</u>, what would that be? **Less work. I'm very worried about the science project. I don't have enough references. I'm concerned about being kicked out of school because I'll get a low grade on it. I got an F on the interim.**

15. Name one easy thing in <u>**science class**</u>. **Remembering the names of things.**

16. What is one thing you are good at in **science class**? **Spelling scientific names. I'm good at spelling.**

17. Do you have any problems with other students in **Mr. Towerman's** class? **Yes.**

18. Which students do you have problems with? **Nathan and sometimes Scott.**

19. Tell me about the problem(s)? **I told you, Nathan calls me names and kicks me. Sometimes Scott does also.**

20. What would help the situation? **If they were far away from me.**

21. Do you always sit in the same seat? **We change seats after every report card.**

22. Do you like where you are sitting? **Yes, except when I'm near Nathan or Scott** Why or why not? (*The student previously specified why, so this question was not asked.*)

23. How does **Mr. Towerman** let you know what the homework is? **He writes it on the board. Sometimes in red. It's hard to read it when it is in red or yellow.** Did you tell him? **I don't want to tell him because the other kids might laugh at me and make fun of my poor eyesight.** (*The interviewer should follow up with school personnel and request that another color be used. It sounds as though this student may be color-blind.*)

24. Does **Mr. Towerman** make any changes that bother you? **Yes, sometimes we are in the middle of something and then he tells us to do something else.**

25. Can you think of anything **Mr. Towerman** does that bothers you? **No.**

26. Are there any things in the classroom that really bother you a lot? (noises, smell, light, temperature etc.) **I don't like the way frogs smell.**

27. Do you have enough time to do what **Mr. Towerman** asks? **Most of the time.**

28. Do you have enough time to switch activities in **science class**? **Not when we switch activities and I haven't finished yet.**

29. Do you have enough time to get your work done? **Sometimes.**

4rd Class

1. What is your **next class** in school? **Language arts.**

2. Who's your teacher? **Mrs. Martin.**

3. Does **Mrs. Martin** notice when you do a good job? **I don't know.**

4. What does **Mrs. Martin** do that tells you you've done a good job? **Nothing.**

5. Do you think **Mrs. Martin** likes you? **I don't know.**

6. What does **Mrs. Martin** do to show you he/she likes you? (*The interviewer did not ask this question because of the answer obtained on the previous question.*)

7. Do you usually work alone or with others? **I heard future projects will need a partner. I did one project with a partner, Collin. I'm doing the current project alone.**

8. What kinds of things do you do alone? **Reading and writing assignments.**

9. What kinds of things do you do with others? **Projects.**

10. Which do you prefer? **Working alone, unless I'm working with Collin.**

11. Is the work difficult or easy? **Spelling definitions are difficult. Projects are difficult. Spelling tests are not just spelling. Have to memorize the definitions. She says it out loud.** (*The interviewer got the idea that perhaps the definitions are read and students have to retrieve the word from hearing the definition. The interviewer would follow up to find out the format of the spelling tests.*) **I had to do a mythology report on a character and there is very little information on him. Other kids are writing reports on guys like Hercules and there is a lot of information on him. This is not fair.**

12. What is the easy part of the schoolwork? **Inserting spelling words into sentences.**

13. What part of schoolwork don't you like in **language arts**?

Writing and spelling definitions, also the mythology report.

14. If you could change one thing about **language arts**, what would that be? **Less writing.**

15. Name one easy thing in **language arts**. **I already told you. Inserting spelling words into sentences.**

16. What is one thing you are good at in **language arts**? (***This question wasn't asked. The interviewer thought he would find the question irritating.***)

17. Do you have any problems with other students in **Mrs. Martin's** class? **No, minus Eric F.**

18. Which students do you have problems with? (***This question was skipped, since he had already indicated who he had difficulty with.***)

19. Tell me about the problem(s)? (***He would not elaborate. In this instance, the interviewer might ask other school personnel if they were aware of an incident between the student and Eric F. The following question was also skipped.***)

20. What would help the situation?

21. Do you always sit in the same seat? **I've moved several time times. The teacher wanted to split up the group. Now I sit alone.**

22. Do you like where you are sitting? **No.** Why or why not? **I'm not happy sitting alone. She made me sit alone because I didn't want to work with anyone else. The rest of the class is working in teams of four and they have four words. I have to do four words alone. That's not fair.** (***The interviewer may want to discuss whether the assignment could be modified to include fewer requirements.***)

23. How does **Mrs. Martin** let you know what the homework is? **She tells us.** (***The interviewer will follow up on this. All homework is to be provided in writing. This is specified on the student's IEP.***)

24. Does **Mrs. Martin** make any changes that bother you? **Yes, seating arrangements.**

25. Can you think of anything **Mrs. Martin** does that bothers you? What? **Just changing the seating**.

26. Are there any things in the classroom that really bother you a lot? (noises, smell, light, temperature etc.) **No.**

27. Do you have enough time to do what **Mrs. Martin** asks? **No.** (*The student may need shortened assignments. Many students with HF-ASD take an inordinately long period of time to produce writing assignments.*)

28. Do you have enough time to switch activities in **language arts**? **I don't know.**

29. Do you have enough time to get your work done? **No, there is too much writing.**

5th Class

1. What is your **next** class in school? **World history.**

2. Who's your teacher? **Mrs. Thompson.**

3. Does **Mrs. Thompson** notice when you do a good job? **Sometimes.**

4. What does **Mrs. Thompson** do that tells you you've done a good job? **I'm not sure.**

5. Do you think **Mrs. Thompson** likes you? **I don't know.**

6. What does **Mrs. Thompson** do to show you she likes you? (*As previously indicated, the answers that the teacher gives do not provide concrete feedback to the student, and the student is unable to read any nonverbal cues regarding how he is doing.*)

7. Do you usually work alone or with others? **Alone.**

8. What kinds of things do you do alone? (*Questions 8 & 9 were skipped, since it appeared as though the student was perfectly comfortable working alone.*)

9. What kinds of things do you do with others? **Nothing.**

10. Which do you prefer? **I like working alone.**

11. Is the work difficult or easy? **Pretty good.**

12. What is the easy part of the schoolwork? **I don't know.**

13. What part of schoolwork don't you like in **world history**?

14. If you could change one thing about **world history class**, what would that be? **One day Mrs. Thompson brought in a cat. I was afraid.**

15. Name one easy thing in **world history** class.

16. What is one thing you are good at in **world history** class?

17. Do you have any problems with other students in **Mrs. Thompson's** class? **No. (*Questions 18-21 were skipped because the student is not reporting problems with other students.*)**

18. Which students do you have problems with?

19. Tell me about the problem(s)?

20. What would help the situation?

21. Do you always sit in the same seat? **Yes.**

22. Do you like where you are sitting? Why or why not? **Yes, it is ok.**

23. How does **Mrs. Thompson** let you know what the homework is? **Tells us. Sometimes I don't hear it and I get a zero. (*As in the previous instance, the interviewer should address this with school personnel.*)**

24. Does **Mrs. Thompson** make any changes that bother you? **No.**

25. Can you think of anything **Mrs. Thompson** does that bothers you? What? **She smells horrible. (*The interviewer should follow up and see if Mrs. Thompson wears perfume. Perhaps the student is particularly sensitive to the smell of her perfume.*)**

26. Are there any things in the classroom that really bother you a lot? (noises, smell, light, temperature etc.) **Mrs. Thompson smells.**

27. Do you have enough time to do what **Mrs. Thompson** asks? **Yes.**

28. Do you have enough time to switch activities in **world history**? **Yes.**

29. Do you have enough time to get your work done? **Yes.**

30. Rank your classes (including bus, lunch) in order with 1 being the best and 7 being the worst, depending on the number of classes/activities that are being rated. (Give the student a list of all classes and activities to include.)

RANK	CLASSES
1	bus
2	lunch
3	computer
4	history
5	math
6	science
7	language arts

31. Rank your teachers and other adults you see at school in order, with 1 being the best and __ being the worst. (Give the student list of teachers and adults to include.)

RANK	TEACHERS' NAMES
1	Inclusion support teacher
2	Special Education coordinator
3	Behavior Specialist
4	Assistant principal
5	Math teacher
6	Computer teacher
7	History teacher
8	Bus driver
9	Science teacher

Bus

32. Who is your bus driver? **Mr. Carl.**

33. Does **Mr. Carl** like you? **Yes.** Dislike you?

34. What does **Mr. Carl** do that tells you he **likes** you? **He always says, "Good morning, Mr. Jay."**

35. Where do you sit on the bus? **Right behind Mr. Carl.**

36. Do you sit near the bus driver? If no, would you like to? *(This question wasn't asked because of the previous answer.)*

37. Do you sit in the same seat every day**? Yes**

38. Does anyone sit in the seat next to you? **Sometimes.** Who? **Emily or Jared.**

39. Are there students on your bus you like? **Yes.** Who? **Emily, Jared, and Scott.**

40. Do you ever talk to them? **Sometimes.**

41. What do you talk about? **Television shows or games.**

42. What do they talk about? **A bunch of different stuff.**

43. Are there students on the bus you do not like? **Yes.** Who? **Two boys who sit farther back.**

44. Why don't you like them? **They yell and push each other.**

45. Do you like riding the bus? **Yes.** Why or why not? (If no, question further) **Mr. Carl is nice to me.** *(Mr. Carl is the morning and afternoon bus driver. It sounds as though the current seating arrangement near Mr. Carl and peers around the student is working out well.)*

Lunch

46. What time do you each lunch? **After science class.**

47. Do you always sit in the same seat? **Usually, there is one broken seat at my table and I try to sit next to that seat.**

48. Who do you like to sit with at lunch? **Collin. Mr. Gary comes by to see me most days.**

49. Is there anyone you do not like to sit with at lunch? **Yes. Who? Nathan, Scott, Eric F. and Miguel.** Why? **They bother me. Mr. Gary makes them sit at another table. If they come over, I am allowed to go to Mr. Gary or Miss Smith and they make them move.**

50. Do you have enough time to eat lunch? **Yes.**

51. Do you like lunchtime? **Yes.**

52. Does the noise in the cafeteria bother you? **Yes, it is really noisy.**

53. Do the smells in the cafeteria bother you? **Yes, some of the smells are disgusting.**

54. If you could change one thing about lunchtime, what would it be? **The noise. If it really bothers me I am allowed to use my pass and go to Mr. Keefe, the counselor's office.**

Appendix D:
Transition Checklist

■ ■ ■

TRANSITION CHECKLIST

Creating a Successful Transition for Students With HF-ASD

Preplanning

Conducting or Reviewing Assessments

☐ Have current school personnel assess the current environment, the student's strength and challenges, as well as necessary supports and accommodations. These will be instrumental in selecting the next environment.

☐ Include staff from the current grade/school *and* those from the next grade or new school in transitional planning meetings.

☐ Ensure that all staff who will be working with the youth understand the student's strengths and concerns.

Choosing Next Environment

☐ Visit different classrooms (if transitioning within the building) or visit types of programs, or programs at different schools (if transitioning to a new building), to determine appropriate placement options.

☐ Hand-pick teachers for the student. Consider selecting teachers who have a direct communication style and explain non-literal terms. These students tend to do well with individuals who are calm, predictable, organized and yet flexible.

☐ Compare similarities and differences between the present and future class/school and to being to identify needed modifications and accommodations.

Transition Planning Meeting

☐ Remember that at each transition, the social ante increases. It is critical to identify and teach expectations and skills prior to the student being expected to exhibit them. Ask staff how a second grade student is different from a third grade student socially. How is a freshman different than a sophomore? Develop a plan to address these issues with the student and parent prior to the transition.

☐ Create the student's schedule. Careful attention should be paid to choosing specials and creating opportunities for "downtime" where the student can engage in preferred activities in order to decrease anxiety levels.

☐ Create, review, and/or revise the IEP or 504 Plan to ensure that all necessary adaptations and modifications are included (i.e., homework, class work, lunch, physical education, before school).

☐ Identify a teacher or administrator who will serve as the primary school contact for the parent to discuss any problems or changes that may occur.

☐ Identify a team of individuals at the school who will serve as "safe person" – someone the student is comfortable talking with about significant issues.

☐ Schedule dates and content of training sessions for school personnel. Some training should be completed before the first day of school and before student orientation. However, it is helpful to provide additional training when staff get to know the student with HF-ASD.

☐ Plan an orientation schedule for the student. Many schools provide a general orientation for all students in the spring. Students with HF-ASD need a more extensive orientation process than typical students. Suggestions for orientation activities are provided under Student Orientation. The majority of the orientation activities may be conducted the weeks before the start of the school year.

Training for School Personnel

☐ Conduct a general orientation for all personnel at the school.

☐ This training session should:

    ☐ Overview the characteristics of individuals with HF-ASD.

    ☐ Provide information on the student's *specific* behavioral, academic, and emotional strengths and concerns.

    ☐ Include all teachers, counselors, administrators, office staff, cafeteria workers, security, etc., who will have contact with the student.

    ☐ Ask the parent to create a one-page synopsis about their child that provides information that may not be obvious, including (a) stress signs, (b) reasons for stress, and (c) suggestions for calming strategies, as well as strengths and interests. Present this at the training meeting.

    ☐ Include enough information about the student with HF-ASD so that staff can engage in positive short dialogues to help the student feel comfortable and supported.

☐ Provide training on how to implement the strategies determined during the transition planning meeting and/or included in the student's IEP or 504 Plan. All teachers, counselors, administrators, and the paraprofessionals who are in contact with the student should be present.

☐ This training session should include information on:

    ☐ The specific, step-by-step procedure the student can use to seek out the safe person and get to home base -- a place where the student can go to escape from the overwhelming environment. The home base typically has items that are self-calming for the individual. It is not escape from work as work goes with the student to home base. She does her work after she is calm.

    ☐ The procedure to be followed for behavioral problems.

    ☐ The procedure for ensuring that homework assignments are recorded and that required materials are brought home.

☐ How to implement all academic modifications, accommodations, and supports.

☐ Any other needs or issues that require discussion.

☐ Provider ongoing training on the student's strengths and needs.

  ☐ Have the student's team complete the Underlying Characteristics Checklist (Aspy & Grossman, 2007) prior to ongoing
  training

  ☐ Use the results of the UCC to create the training sessions.

Student Orientation

☐ Encourage the student to keyboard or dictate a letter to the
administrator about the transition. This letter should include
what the student is excited about, what they are nervous
about and how they can be helped to transition. This is a great
first step to supporting self-advocacy.

☐ Provide several walk-throughs of the student's daily schedule.
In schools where the schedule changes from day to day, the
student should have the opportunity to practice all possible
schedules. If applicable, student "buddies" should be available
to walk through the schedule with the student with HF-ASD.
The following are suggestions for the walk-through:

  ☐ Provide visual/written class schedule(s) for the student.

  ☐ Videotape a practice walk-through school schedule for the
  student to review at home.

  ☐ Practice route(s) from various classes to the bathroom,
  counselor's office, home base, etc.

  ☐ Meet all teachers and relevant personnel.

  ☐ Provide the student with pictures and names of all teachers
  in advance of the orientation.

  ☐ Provide the student with pictures and names of all support
  personnel, such as safe person, counselors, special education coordinators, assistant principals and principal in
  advance of the orientation.

☐ Provide the student with pictures and names of all additional personnel, such as cafeteria workers, school nurse, etc.

☐ Provide the student with pictures and names of student "buddies."

☐ Show the student where her assigned seat in each classroom will be.

☐ Obtain information about school routines and rules (i.e., lunch, rules about going to bathroom, before/after school, transportation).

☐ Practice routines, such as finding homeroom from the bus stop, opening the locker, going through the cafeteria line, etc.

☐ Provide instruction on the procedure for seeking out the safe person and home base.

☐ Practice use of transition to home base through role-play.

Academic Modifications

Priming

☐ Determine whether priming will help meet the student's need for predictability.

☐ Analyze student needs and classroom demands to determine which classes will require priming.

☐ Identify who will prime.

☐ Designate whether priming will use actual or similar materials.

☐ Determine where and when priming will occur.

Classroom Assignments

☐ Determine the student's needs concerning assignments.

☐ Provide the student with extra time to complete assignments.

☐ Shorten the length of assignments.

☐ Reduce the number of assignments.

☐ Break assignments into smaller segments.

☐ Provide samples/models of completed assignments and/or a list of specific criteria for successful completion.

☐ Allow the student to use the computer for schoolwork and/or homework.

☐ Allow the student to demonstrate mastery of concepts through alternate means (dictate essays, oral tests, etc.).

Note-Taking

☐ Indicate the type of note-taking supports needed by the student.

☐ Provide a complete outline.

☐ Give student a skeletal outline.

☐ Identify a peer who can take notes for the student.

☐ Allow child to use outlining software.

Graphic Organizers

☐ Determine whether graphic organizers are needed to facilitate skill acquisition and maintenance.

☐ Specify which type of graphic organizers will be needed:

    ☐ Hierarchical

    ☐ Conceptual

    ☐ Sequential

    ☐ Cyclical

    ☐ Other

☐ Determine who will construct and provide organizer to student:

    ☐ Teacher

    ☐ Peer

    ☐ Student with template

    ☐ Student with outlining software

Enrichment

☐ Determine the type of enrichment needed.

☐ Specify how the enrichment area will be identified.

☐ Determine when and how enrichment will be provided.

☐ Decide whether a learning contract with specified working conditions is needed.

Homework

☐ Identify which class subjects will include homework responsibilities.

☐ Determine homework modifications.

☐ Present homework assignments visually (on board, etc.) in addition to orally.

☐ Provide the student with a homework sheet or planner.

☐ Provide peer or teacher assistance in recording homework assignments.

☐ Provide student with the assignment in written format.

☐ Reduce the amount of homework.

☐ Provide a study hall period to allow the student time to complete homework at school.

☐ Identify home strategy for completing homework.

☐ Designate place and time for homework completion.

☐ Define organization to get homework back to school.

☐ Name contact if additional clarification is needed on homework.

Modifications for Less Structured or Unstructured Times of the Day

Transportation/Bus

☐ Identify who will teach the student the bus routine.

☐ Determine who will provide assistance for the student when the bus arrives at school, particularly on the first day of school. Have a peer or school person greet the student at the bus and accompany him to the bus at the end of the day.

☐ Determine how long assistance will be needed in getting to and from the bus throughout the school year.

☐ Identify the peer or school personnel to be assigned to assist the student in this process, backups.

☐ Provide a pickup or dropoff closer to the student's house.

☐ Provide adult supervision at the bus stop.

☐ Provide a peer "buddy" from the student's neighborhood to wait with the student at the bus stop and sit with the student on the bus.

☐ Provide preferential seating on the bus. This may include seating the student in close proximity to the driver or allowing her to sit in her own seat/row.

☐ Provide a monitor or aide on the bus.

☐ Provide a special bus.

Physical Education

☐ Consider whether to exempt the student from physical education and, if so, substitute another special or a study hall. This is particularly important if poor motor skills have led to teasing or rejection by peers.

☐ Assign the student a specific role for PE such as scorekeeper, equipment manager, etc. This allows him to participate in PE, but minimizes the motor and social demands of playing a sport.

☐ Assign teams rather than allow students to choose teams themselves.

☐ Have school personnel monitor, at least twice weekly, the student's perceptions of the PE period by asking her how she feels the period is going.

☐ Help the student problem-solve difficulties.

Lunch

☐ Have school personnel available during the first week of school to assist the student in navigating the cafeteria line, finding a place to sit, and engaging in an appropriate activity once he has finished eating.

☐ Help the student identify school personnel that she can approach during the lunch period when encountering problems.

☐ Have school personnel closely monitor the student's interactions with peers and intervene when problems occur.

☐ Have school personnel closely monitor the student and intervene when the student becomes stressed and overwhelmed or begins to experience sensory overload.

☐ Have school personnel monitor, at least twice weekly, the student's perceptions of the lunch period by asking the student how he/she feels the period is going.

☐ Help the student problem-solve any difficulties.

☐ Provide assigned seating with a preferred friend, away from problem peers and/or near adult supervision.

☐ Provide a peer "buddy/buddies" during lunchtime.

☐ Allow the student to leave the cafeteria once he has finished eating, to engage in a calming or preferred activity (e.g., go to media center, computer lab).

☐ Allow the student to eat lunch in an alternative location if necessary (e.g., counselor's office, media center).

Changing Classes

☐ Provide peer or teacher assistance (particularly during the first week of school) to help the student manage the crowded hallways, open locker, locate the proper materials, and find the correct classroom.

☐ Provide a peer "buddy" to accompany the student during class changes if he continues to experience difficulty during this time. This "buddy" might assist the student with organizational issues, protect against teasing/bullying by other students, and help promote positive social interactions.

☐ Provide the student with additional time for class changes.

☐ Allow alternate passing time when the hallways are free from other students. For example, the student might change classes before or after the general transition period.

Changes in Routine

☐ Specify whether the student needs to be informed of any changes in typical classroom procedures (assemblies, fire drills, guest speakers, seating changes, substitute teacher).

☐ Determine what additional supports the student needs when changes occur.

Before and After School

☐ Identify when the student should arrive at school.

☐ Determine whether a specific room should be used during this time.

☐ Identify peers to support the student at this time.

☐ Provide structured activities.

Environmental Supports

Preferential Seating

☐ Determine if preferential seating is necessary and provide.

☐ Identify peers who can support student.

Organizational Strategies

☐ Determine the student's needs concerning organization of papers and materials.

☐ Provide assistance in organizing the backpack, locker, and/or desk and teach the student to do so independently.

☐ Teach the student to use timelines.

☐ Instruct the student on how to develop a to-do list.

Rules and Routines

☐ Provide visual supports to teach rules and routines in *each* classroom.

☐ Provide direction instruction and practices on all rules and routines.

Home Base

☐ Identify whether the student needs a home base -- a place to escape an overwhelming environment or prepare for a potentially stressful upcoming event.

☐ Identify when home base will be used:

  ☐ Before school or early morning

  ☐ Following specific classes

  ☐ At the end of the day

☐ Determine cue to prompt home base.

☐ Determine home base location.

☐ Identify activities that will occur during home base.

☐ Identify who should monitor the home base.

☐ Determine whether a peer buddy or adult should accompany the student to the home base.

Safe Person

☐ Identify a safe person (one who knows the student and can help in the event that the student becomes overwhelmed or confused.

☐ Determine the role of the safe person. (This person may serve as an unobtrusive facilitator and social interpreter to help the student with social, communication, and academic skills. This person may also serve as a resource for other staff members and as a liaison with the family. In middle/high school, a "team" of individuals who can serve as a safe person may be needed.) The safe person can provide:

    ☐ Social skills training

    ☐ Social skills interpretation

    ☐ Active listening

    ☐ Calming strategies

    ☐ Sensory supports, including earbuds or headphones that can be worn in hallways, cafeteria, or other busy environments

Visual Supports

☐ Identify which supports are needed, including:

    ☐ Map of school outlining classes

    ☐ List of classes, room numbers, books, and other supplies

    ☐ List of teacher expectations and routines for each class

    ☐ Outlines and notes from lectures

- ☐ Model of assignments
- ☐ Test reminders
- ☐ Schedule changes
- ☐ Homework
- ☐ Cue to use home base

Travel Card (see Appendix E)

- ☐ Identify special educator role.
- ☐ Determine student role.
- ☐ Identify general educator participation.
- ☐ Define parent role.

Social Supports

Teachers

- ☐ Develop an alternative plan when there will be a substitute teacher.
- ☐ Assess teacher's language and nonverbal communication.
- ☐ Write social narratives to help the student understand teachers' styles.

Hidden Curriculum

- ☐ Identify hidden curriculum items.
- ☐ Define who will teach hidden curriculum.
- ☐ Determine when instruction will occur.

Circle of Friends/Lunch Bunch

- ☐ Provide awareness training to peers.

☐ Identify peers to participate in Circle of Friends/Lunch Bunch/ Peer Buddies.

☐ Determine when Circle of Friends/Lunch Bunch/Peer Buddies are needed for support.

Social Skills Instruction

☐ Determine need for direct instruction.

☐ Identify curricula.

☐ Determine social skills instructor.

☐ Determine when social skills instruction will occur.

☐ Determine if acting lessons may support social skills instruction.

☐ Identify coach's need for HF-ASD awareness training.

☐ Provide awareness training to other student actors.

☐ Consider whether social stories are a viable means of instruction.

☐ Identify individual who can create social narratives.

☐ Determine how the need for a social narrative will be communicated.

☐ Determine who will monitor social narrative effectiveness.

Social Skills Interpretation

☐ Determine social skills interpreter.

☐ Ensure social skills interpreter knows how to use (a) cartooning, (b) social autopsies, (c) SOCCSS, and (d) sensory awareness.

☐ Identify when student will have access to the social skills interpreter:

　☐ Scheduled time

　☐ As needed

Adapted From Myles, B. S. ,& Adreon, D. (2001). *Asperger syndrome and adolescence; Practical solu-tions for school success.* Reprinted with permission.

Appendix E:
The Travel Card

■ ■ ■

Travel Card

The Travel Card, first discussed by Jones and Jones (1995), is designed to (a) increase productive behavior in adolescents with AS across their many environments, (b) facilitate collaboration between teachers, (c) increase awareness among teachers of the goals the student is working on, and (d) improve home-school communication. Briefly, across the top the Travel Card lists four to five target behaviors the student is working on with a listing of the classes the student attends along the left-hand side. At the end of each period, the teacher indicates whether the student performed the desired behaviors by marking a + (yes), 0 (no), or NA (not applicable) on the card.

At the end of the day, the positive notations are tallied and graphed. Points are accumulated toward a menu of reinforcers that have been jointly negotiated by the student and the adult responsible for the Travel Card. Initially, it is recommended that Travel Cards be used four days a week, with the fifth day used for reinforcement. The student may elect to receive a reinforcer right away or opt to place the points into a Travel Account that can be redeemed at a later time. Additional information on the Travel Card may be found in *Asperger Syndrome and Adolescence: Practical Solutions for School Success* by Adreon and Myles (2001).

Contributed by Laura B. Carpenter, Auburn University, Montgomery.

Travel Card

Date	
Name	

	TARGET BEHAVIORS				
Classes	**Target 1**	**Target 2**	**Target 3**	**Target 4**	**Teacher's initials**

Bonus Points	For	Points	For	Points

Total	+

Teacher Comments/Suggestions/Announcements:

SAMPLE COMPLETED

Travel Card

Date	4/15
Name	Rocky

Classes	TARGET BEHAVIORS				
	Follow Class Rules	Participate in Class	Complete Assignments	Turn in Homework	Teacher's initials
Literacy	X	X	X	X	JK
Science		X	X		LH
Study Skills	X	X	X	X	NO
Social Studies		X	X		PQ
Spanish	X	X	X	X	RS
Social Skills	X	X	X	X	TU

Bonus Points	Went to nurse after getting off bus	Points 5	Has assignment notebook	Points 5

Total	+110

Teacher Comments/Suggestions/Announcements:

Printed in the USA
CPSIA information can be obtained
at www.ICGtesting.com
JSHW011912050823
46023JS00003B/14